SACRED READINGS

Sacred Readings

A JOURNAL

Kenneth Boa

NAVPRESS

BRINGING TRUTH TO LIFE

P.O. Box 35001, Colorado Springs, Colorado 80935

The Navigators is an international Christian organization. Our mission is to reach, disciple, and equip people to know Christ and to make Him known through successive generations. We envision multitudes of diverse people in the United States and every other nation who have a passionate love for Christ, live a lifestyle of sharing Christ's love, and multiply spiritual laborers among those without Christ.

NavPress is the publishing ministry of The Navigators. NavPress publications help believers learn biblical truth and apply what they learn to their lives and ministries. Our mission is to stimulate spiritual formation among our readers.

The introductory material in this journal was adapted from the section on devotional spirituality in Kenneth Boa's book, *Conformed to His Image* (Grand Rapids: Zondervan Publishing House, 2001), with permission of the publishers.

Cover design by Dan Jamison
Cover Calligraphy by Don Bishop/Artville
Cover Photo by Zephyr Images
Creative Team: Jacqueline Eaton Blakley, Lori Mitchell, iDesignEtc.

Boa, Kenneth.
        Sacred readings : a journal / Kenneth Boa.
            p. cm.
        Contents: v. 1. Selected biblical passages.
        ISBN 1-57683-211-2
            1. Bible—Reading. 2. Bible—Devotional use. 3. Devotional calendars.
4. Spiritual life—Christianity. I. Title.

BS617 .B63 2000
248.4'6—dc21

                                                                        00-035499

Printed in the United States of America

1 2 3 4 5 6 7 8 9 10 / 05 04 03 02 01 00

Inside This Journal

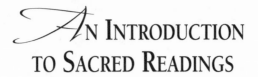

An Introduction to Sacred Readings

OUR IMAGE OF GOD

There is but one God, the Father, from whom are all things, and we exist for Him; and one Lord, Jesus Christ, by whom are all things, and we exist through Him.

—1 Corinthians 8:6

We do not exist for ourselves—we exist *for* the Father and *through* the Son. The world tells us that we derive our existence from it and that we should live for ourselves, but the Word teaches us that all we are and have comes from the Father who formed us for His pleasure and purposes.

Ultimate reality is not the cosmos or a mysterious force, but an infinite and loving Person. The implications of this are astounding and pervasive. The infinite-personal Lord of all is an unbounded loving community of three timeless and perfect Persons. In the superabundance of His joy and life, He is at once solitude and society, the one and the many, supernal being as communion. The magnificent God who abounds in personal plenitude has no needs, yet He invites us to participate in the intense and interpenetrating life of the three eternally subsistent Selves. Jesus prayed on our behalf "that they may all be one; even as You, Father, are in Me and I in You, that they also may be in Us. . . . I in them and You in Me, that they may be perfected in unity, so that the world may know that You sent Me, and loved them, even as You have loved Me" (John 17:21, 23). The impenetrable mystery of us being in the divine Us, and the divine Us being in us, transcends our imagination— but if it is true, all else pales in comparison.

Devotional spirituality revels in the glorious attributes of God and aspires to lay hold of God's aspiration for us. It prepares our souls for the "mystic sweet communion" of living entirely in God and in one another as the three Persons of God eternally live and rejoice in one another. It instills in us a passion for Christ's indwelling life and inspires us to swim in the river of torrential love that flows from His throne of grace.

In 1677, Henry Scougal observed in his little book, *The Life of God in the Soul of Man,* that "The worth and excellency of a soul is to be measured by the object of its love." Our souls become emaciated when their pleasure is affixed to position, possessions, and power, because these things are destined to corrupt and perish. But as we gradually (and often painfully) transfer our affections from the created and finite world to the uncreated and infinite Maker of the world, our souls become great and glorious. As we take the risk of seeking God's pleasure above our own, we discover the ironic byproduct of a greater satisfaction and contentment than if we sought these things as ends in themselves. As we learn to fix our eyes on Jesus, not for His benefits but *for Himself*, we find that we have all things in Him.

Scripture teaches us that we steadily become conformed to what we most love and admire. *We become like our focus;* as we behold the glory of the Lord, we are being "transformed into the same image from glory to glory, just as from the Lord, the Spirit" (2 Corinthians 3:18). We gradually come to resemble what we worship. But if our heart's desire is fixed on something in this world, it becomes idolatrous and soul-corrupting. Hosea declared that the people of Israel "became as detestable as that which they loved" (Hosea 9:10). But when we turn the focus of our love away from the idols of this world system to the beauty of Christ, we discover the liberty of the Spirit of the Lord. If we draw our life from loving communion with the caring, radiant, majestic, and unfathomable Being who formed us for Himself, our souls become noble as they grow in conformity to His character.

GOD'S WORLD, HIS WORD, HIS WORKS, AND HIS WAYS

God in His inner essence is a mystery beyond our comprehension; we will never know Him as He knows Himself. The great pilgrims along the way have discovered that progress from superficial to substantive apprehension of God is not so much a movement from darkness to light as it is a plummeting into the ever-increasing profundity of the cloud of unknowing. Kallistos Ware in *The Orthodox Way* distinguishes the *essence* of God and the *energies* of God. In His essence, God is radically transcendent, but in His energies, He is immanent and omnipresent. As Ware notes, "The Godhead is simple and indivisible, and has no parts. The essence signifies the whole God as he is in himself; the energies signify the whole God as he is in action. God in his entirety is completely present in each of his divine energies." As we reflect on the way God reveals Himself, we come to know Him more clearly, and this enables us to love Him more dearly, and to follow Him more nearly. God makes Himself known to us through His world, His Word, His works, and His ways.

Loving God Through His World

> *The heavens are telling of the glory of God; and their expanse is declaring the work of His hands.*
>
> —Psalm 19:1

> *O Lord, how many are Your works! In wisdom You have made them all; the earth is full of Your possessions.*
>
> —Psalm 104:24

8

Read Psalm 19:1-6 and Psalms 104 and 148 carefully and prayerfully, and you will be struck by the manifold ways in which God designed the heavens and earth to display His glory, wisdom, and greatness.

Meditation on the created order is too often neglected as a meaningful component of devotional spirituality. This is unfortunate, because creation abounds with resplendent wonders on every order of magnitude from the microcosm to the macrocosm that point beyond themselves to the beauty and unimaginable brilliance of the Creator of the cosmos. Consider these marvels of order and design: particles and atoms, light and colors, microbes and diatoms, snowflakes, insects, seeds, flowers, leaves, shells, rocks and minerals, fruits, vegetables, plants, small and large birds, small and large fish, whales, small and large animals, trees, mountains, clouds, weather, the seasons, our earth, the planets, stars, nebulae, our galaxy, clusters and super-clusters of galaxies.

You formed my inward parts; You wove me in my mother's womb.
I will give thanks to You, for I am fearfully and wonderfully
made; wonderful are Your works, and my soul knows it very well.
—Psalm 139:13-14

Of all God's created works, the human body best displays God's creative skill and design. I recommend two books that will help you worship God by reflecting on the marvels of the human and spiritual body: *Fearfully and Wonderfully Made* and *In His Image* by Dr. Paul Brand and Philip Yancey. These books portray the way physical systems like cells, bone, skin, motion, blood, the head, and the sensation of pain teach spiritual truth.

Let me mention two things that have helped me love God through His world. The first is an occasional trip to special places where I am encompassed in the natural order. In such places I sometimes sit back and stare at the stars until I realize that I am no longer looking up, but also *down*, and that I am wholly enveloped by the splendor and grandeur of the heavens. An experience like this is humbling because it dramatically shifts my perspective and reminds me that apart from God and His grace, I am nothing. I gain a similar sense of awe by looking at recent photographs of star clouds and distant galaxies. The veritable explosion in scientific knowledge in our time gives us access to new avenues of appreciating God that were never before available.

The second thing I use to stimulate wonder is a set of field lenses and a miniature high-intensity flashlight. I use this "nature kit" from time to time to observe otherwise invisible colors and patterns in flowers, insects, rocks, and so forth. The very act of slowing down enough to observe and appreciate the rich intricacy and diversity of the created order is a healthy exercise in recollection and renewal.

There is no limit to the images and insights that can be gleaned from nature if we take the time and have the eyes to see. We would do well to cultivate a childlike sense of amazement and awe at the things we tend to overlook every day. Our artificial environments and busy schedules make us forget that we are surrounded by mystery and majesty. I encourage you to make the effort to enjoy more frequent and deliberate contact with God's creation and to develop a deeper appreciation for the complexity, beauty, and resplendence of the heavens and the earth. As you do this, you will sense that the God who designed all this and spoke it into being is utterly competent, trustworthy, and lovable.

Loving God Through His Word

Open my eyes, that I may behold wonderful things from Your law.
—Psalm 119:18

The Word of God restores the soul, imparts wisdom, gives joy to the heart, enlightens the eyes, reveals God's righteousness, and endures forever.
—Psalm 19:7-9

Scripture was revealed not merely to inform us, but to transform us. In *Shaped by the Word*, M. Robert Mulholland Jr. contrasts two approaches to Scripture:

INFORMATIONAL READING	FORMATIONAL READING
Seeks to cover as much as possible	Focuses on small portions
A linear process	An in-depth process
Seeks to master the text	Allows the text to master us
The text as an object to use	The text as a subject that shapes us
Analytical, critical, and judgmental approach	Humble, detached, willing, loving approach
Problem-solving mentality	Openness to mystery

There is an important place for informational reading of Scripture and for exegetical and topical methods of Bible study. But those who approach Scripture only in this way often overlook the formational approach that centers on speaking to the heart more than informing the mind. The Bible is not merely an object, but a divinely inspired oracle that is "living and active" (Hebrews 4:12) and has the power to transform those who receive it in humility and obedience (James 1:21-22). Devotional spirituality stresses the formative power of revealed truth and encourages us to love God through His Word. We will look at a time-tested method of doing this in the pages ahead.

Loving God Through His Works

> *Say to God, "How awesome are Your works!"*
> *Come and see the works of God,*
> *Who is awesome in His deeds toward the sons of men.*
> *I shall remember the deeds of the Lord;*
> *Surely I will remember Your wonders of old.*
> *I will meditate on all Your work*
> *And muse on Your deeds.*
> *You are the God who works wonders;*
> *You have made known Your strength among the peoples.*
> *You have by Your power redeemed Your people.*
>
> —Psalms 66:3,5; 77:11-12,14-15

The psalmists frequently reviewed and reflected upon God's historical acts of redemption, protection, and provision. Both Testaments abound with accounts of how God has worked in specific and dramatic ways in the lives of people and in the destiny of nations. He has demonstrated His just and loving purposes in the arena of human history, and prayerful consideration of His mighty works of creation, redemption, and consummation is another way of enhancing our worship and devotion for the triune Godhead.

> *Worthy are You, our Lord and our God, to receive glory and*
> *honor and power; for You created all things, and because of Your*
> *will they existed, and were created. . . . Worthy are You to take*
> *the book and to break its seals; for You were slain, and purchased*
> *for God with Your blood men from every tribe and tongue and*
> *people and nation. You have made them to be a kingdom and*
> *priests to our God; and they will reign upon the earth. . . . Wor-*
> *thy is the Lamb that was slain to receive power and riches and*
> *wisdom and might and honor and glory and blessing. . . . To Him*
> *who sits on the throne, and to the Lamb, be blessing and honor*
> *and glory and dominion forever and ever.*
>
> —Revelation 4:11; 5:9-10,12-13

Loving God Through His Ways

> *He made known His ways to Moses, His acts to the sons of Israel.*
>
> —Psalm 103:7

Moses not only knew the Lord through His works, but he also knew and loved the Lord through His ways. God's ways concern His personal involvement in our lives and our experiences of His peace, power, provision, protection, compassion, and care. It is good to build a "personal history" of God's providential care by reviewing and remembering the things He has done at various points along your spiritual journey. Remember His surprising answers to prayer, the way He drew you to Himself, the way He carried you through turbulent waters, the way He provided for your needs when circumstances looked hopeless, the way He encouraged and comforted you in your distress, the way He exhorted you through others and disciplined you for your good, and the way He seeks to strip you of your hope in the things of this world so that you will learn to hope only in Him.

> *Come and hear, all who fear God,*
> *And I will tell of what He has done for my soul.*
> *Certainly God has heard;*
> *He has given heed to the voice of my prayer.*
> *Blessed be God,*
> *Who has not turned away my prayer*
> *Nor His lovingkindness from me.*
> *Your way, O God, is holy;*
> *What god is great like our God?*
>
> —Psalm 66:16,19-20; 77:13

I will tell of what He has done for my soul. Grateful reflection on what God has done for your soul is a vital component of devotional spirituality.

God's ways also relate to the multifaceted attributes of His person, powers, and perfection. Because our capacity to love God is related to our image of God, we do well to pray for the grace of growing in understanding of the glories of His attributes: His unlimited power, presence, and knowledge; His holiness, justice, goodness, truthfulness, and righteousness; His goodness, grace, compassion, mercy, and love; His beauty, glory, greatness, transcendent majesty, and dominion; and His self-existence, eternity, infinity, and immutability. As Dallas Willard puts it in *The Divine Conspiracy*, God is "an interlocking community of magnificent persons, completely self-sufficing and with no meaningful limits on goodness and power." He is the absolute answer to the perennial quest for the true, the good, and the beautiful.

THE PRACTICE OF SACRED READING

The ancient art of sacred reading (*lectio divina*) centers on loving God through His Word. It was introduced to the West by the Eastern desert father John Cassian early in the fifth century. The sixth-century Rule of St. Benedict that guided Benedictine and Cistercian monastic practice, prescribed daily periods for sacred reading. Unfortunately, by the end of the Middle Ages it came to be seen as a method that should be restricted to the spiritually elite. As time passed, even monastics lost the simplicity of sacred reading as it was replaced by more complicated systems and forms of "mental prayer." In recent decades, however, this ancient practice has been revitalized, especially by those in the Cistercian tradition. Writers like Thomas Merton (*Contemplative Prayer, New Seeds of Contemplation, Spiritual Direction & Meditation*), Thomas Keating (*Intimacy with God, Open Mind, Open Heart*), Michael Casey (*Sacred Reading, Toward God, The Undivided Heart*), and Thelma Hall (*Too Deep for Words*) have been promoting sacred reading in Catholic circles, and Protestants are now being exposed to this approach as well. Sacred reading, or *lectio divina*, involves a progression through the four movements of reading, meditation, prayer, and contemplation.

READING (LECTIO)

In his study of monastic culture, *The Love of Learning and the Desire for God*, Jean Leclercq distinguished two distinct approaches to Scripture that were used in the Middle Ages. While medieval universities were urban schools that prepared clerics for the active life, rural monasteries focused on spiritual formation within a liturgical framework to equip monks for the contemplative life. The scholastics approached Scripture by focusing on the page of sacred text (*sacra pagina*) as an object to be studied and investigated by putting questions to the text (*quaestio*) and by questioning oneself with the subject matter (*disputatio*). By contrast, the monastics approached Scripture through a personal orientation of meditation (*meditatio*) and prayer (*oratio*). While the scholastics sought science and knowledge in the text, the monastics sought wisdom and appreciation. Those in the schools were more oriented to the objective, the theological, and the cognitive; those in the cloisters were more oriented to the subjective, the devotional, and the affective.

Most contemporary approaches to Bible study have more in common with the scholastics than with the monastics. Recalling a distinction we made earlier, they are more concerned with informational reading than with formational reading. There is a legitimate need for both approaches, since an overemphasis on one or the other can lead to the extremes of cold intellectualism or mindless enthusiasm. But when evangelicals study Scripture, they typically look more for precepts and principles than for an encounter with God in the depths of their being. The practice of *lectio divina* can correct this lack of balance, because it stresses the reading of Scripture for spiritual formation through receptive openness to God's loving call of grace. *Lectio* is not an intellectual exercise that seeks to control and to gather information, but a voluntary immersion in the Word of God that seeks to receive and to respond. Spiritual reading melds revelation with experience. It is done in the spirit of the collect for the second Sunday in Advent in the 1928 *Book of Common Prayer*:

Blessed Lord, who hast caused all holy Scriptures to be written for our learning; Grant that we may in such wise hear them, read, mark, learn, and inwardly digest them, that by patience and comfort of thy holy Word, we may embrace, and ever hold fast, the blessed hope of everlasting life, which thou hast given us in our Saviour Jesus Christ.

May we learn to hear the holy Scriptures and to "read, mark, learn, and inwardly digest" them.

Suggestions for Reading

- Choose a special place (preferably away from your desk and other areas of activity) that is suitable for this purpose. Sanctify this space by reserving it as a regular meeting place with the Lord.
- Choose a special time in which you can be alert and consistent. Invite God to lead you to rearrange your life to allow more time with Him. This will be more a matter of *making* time rather than finding time. Making time for this purpose is a response to God's calling in a world of constant external demands. Although this will not work for everyone, I recommend exchanging the last hour of the night for an extra hour in the morning. (Most of us could redeem a significant amount of time by reducing and being more selective in our intake of television.) Whenever it is, give God your best time, when you are least sluggish, and when you can be quiet, still, and unpressured by outward hindrances.
- Consistency is critical, since there will be many temptations to postpone and neglect sacred reading. The benefits of *lectio* are attained gradually over a long-term process.
- Because *lectio divina* engages the whole person, your bodily posture is important. A seated position that is erect but not tense or slouched is best for the four movements of *lectio*. It is good to be fully attentive and alert without sitting in a way that will eventually impede your circulation or breathing.
- Try to be systematic in the way you select your Scripture texts. They can emerge from a daily Bible reading program or through the use of a lectionary that gives you daily Old Testament, gospel, and epistle readings. Or your passages can come out of a devotional guide. (I often use my *Handbook to Prayer* and *Handbook to Renewal* for this purpose.)
- To avoid distraction in sacred reading, it is better to use a Bible without study notes. Use an accurate translation rather than a paraphrase (I use the updated edition of the NASB) for *lectio divina*.
- Keep the passage brief—do not confuse quantity with quality.
- It is also helpful to apply this method of slow, deliberate, and prayerful reading to other resources such as the creeds, traditional and patristic texts, and classic spiritual books. Samples of some of these resources

14

are available in *Devotional Classics*, edited by Richard J. Foster and James Bryan Smith. Older literature has a way of challenging the biases of our modern presuppositions, if we will let it seep into us.

- Begin with a prayer of preparation: for example, "Open my eyes, that I may behold wonderful things from Your law" (Psalm 119:18), or, "Let the words of my mouth and the meditation of my heart be acceptable in Your sight, O Lord, my Rock and my Redeemer" (Psalm 19:14). Start with a clear intention to know God's will for your life and a fixed resolution in advance to do it.

- Slowly read the text again and again until it is in your short-term memory. Try making your first readings audible, since this will make them slower and more deliberate. (Bear in mind that in antiquity, reading always meant reading aloud.)

- Seek the meaning of the text; ask questions. But come more as a disciple than as a collector of information. See Scripture as iconographic; that is, a verbal window into the reality of life that turns your perspective around.

- Listen to the words in humility accompanied by a willingness to obey. Hearing the Word must be united by faith (Hebrews 4:2) with an intention to apply it in practice (James 1:22). Open yourself to be addressed by the Word in your attitudes, habits, choices, and emotions. There will be times when you resist a penetrating living encounter with God, and these generally have to do with areas of disobedience. Thus, it is wise to examine your being and doing in the light of the text by asking, *Lord, what are You saying to me in this passage?*

- Remember that unlike ordinary reading, in *lectio* you are seeking to be *shaped* by the Word more than *informed* by the Word. This first step of reading prepares you for the remaining three movements of meditation, prayer, and contemplation. But the whole process should be infused with a prayerful attitude.

- Avoid the usual pragmatic reflex that seeks to "net out" some immediate benefit. Approach sacred reading with no conditions, demands, or expectations. The Word may not meet your perceived needs, but it will touch your real needs, even when you don't discern them.

MEDITATION (MEDITATIO)

As you move from reading to meditation, you are seeking to saturate and immerse yourself in the Word, to luxuriate in its living waters, and to receive the words as an intimate and personal message from God. The purpose of meditation is to penetrate the Scriptures and to let them penetrate us through the loving gaze of the heart. The term *mental prayer* is often associated with meditation, but this could be misleading, because *lectio, meditatio,* and *oratio* involve not only the mind, but also the heart. Meditation attunes the inward self to the Holy Spirit so that our hearts harmonize and resonate with His voice. Meditation is a spiritual work of holy desire and an interior invitation for the Spirit to pray and speak within us (Romans 8:26-27) in such a way that our whole being is transformed into greater conformity with Jesus Christ. It is an intentional process of building our passion for Christ by meeting with Him and spending time with Him to know Him more clearly, to love Him more dearly, and to follow Him more nearly. By meditating on God's truth, we are inviting Christ to be formed in us (Galatians 4:19) by a deliberate dwelling on His words. Thus, mental prayer should not be seen as an abstract exercise but as a vital vehicle for the metamorphosis of the soul.

> *This book of the law shall not depart from your mouth, but you shall meditate on it day and night, so that you may be careful to do according to all that is written in it; for then you will make your way prosperous, and then you will have success.*
>
> —Joshua 1:8

This familiar verse tells us that the path to success *as God defines it* is the habit of making space in our lives to meet with God in His holy Word with a heartfelt intention to apply what He reveals through obedient action. Only ;those who delight in God's Word and habitually meditate on it (Psalm 1:2) will experience the fullness and stability of God's purpose and calling. May you be one of them.

Suggestions for Meditation

- Since it is God's love for us that teaches us to love Him, we should not regard meditation as an objective method or technique, but as a person-specific process. It is good to experiment with different approaches until you find a pattern of meditation that resonates best with your soul.
- Acknowledge the holiness of the God you are approaching and the richness of the gift of faith that makes it possible for you to enjoy an encounter with Him through His Spirit.
- Meditation is a long-term process that builds upon itself. The more we absorb Scripture, the greater our mental storehouse becomes. As this process continues for months and years, we experience the phenomenon of *reminiscence* in which a word or phrase spontaneously evokes a wealth of imagery from other parts of Scripture. This can be an exciting and creative experience in which we see connections and rhythms we never perceived before. These chain reactions, the fruit of habitual meditation, develop "the mind of Christ" in us (1 Corinthians 2:16).
- Allow enough time to enjoy the text; to rush this process is like running through a great art gallery.
- Meditation on Scripture involves ruminating (*ruminatio*) on a word, phrase, passage, or story. When we chew on the text in our minds, we

release the full flavor as we assimilate its content.

- Don't force meditation or make impatient demands of immediate gratification and results. Meditation will do you little good if you try to control the outcome.
- When you encounter something that speaks particularly to you, you should note it so that you can reflect on it later. You may find it helpful to make written reminders that you can carry with you.
- It may also be beneficial to keep a journal of your personal reflections on the text. If you do this, you will need to be open and honest with yourself in the things you record. The advantage of a journal is the creation of a private record that can be reviewed from time to time.
- Personalize the words of the text and "real-ize" them; receive them as God speaking to you in the present moment. Try to hear the passage as though for the first time, personally addressed to you.
- When a passage speaks to you, consider meditating on the same text for several days before moving on to another.
- The millions of images we have been exposed to through television, movies, magazines, newspapers, and other media have not sharpened but dulled our creative imagination. More than ever, we need to develop and sanctify our imagination, because the truth of Scripture and spiritual experience is, to use Jean Leclercq's words, "impregnated with a mysterious light impossible to analyze." A sanctified imagination will enable us to grasp more than we can see, but we need the lifeline of Scripture to tether us to the truth.
- Many people have found it helpful to engage the five senses when meditating on biblical stories, especially the stories in the Gospels. This process makes the scene more present and real to us and it helps us transition from the cognitive, analytical level to the affective, feeling level of our being.
- In addition to the imaginative use of the senses, it can be illuminating to put yourself in the story. How would you have reacted, and what would you have thought and said if you were there?
- The *Spiritual Exercises* of Ignatius of Loyola incorporates these and other meditative techniques and has useful insights on contemplating the incarnation, life, death, resurrection, and ascension of Christ. The various meditations and prayers prescribed in *Introduction to the Devout Life* by Francis de Sales (on such topics as our creation, the end for which we were created, sin, death, humility, and God's love for us) are also valuable resources for many. But because temperaments differ, not everyone will find such methodical meditation schemes helpful. Most people are sensory, but some are more analytical, and others are more intuitive. Intuitives will benefit more from savoring the truths of a passage than from its imagery. To quote Dom Chapman, "Pray as you can, not as you can't!"

- Meditation on the Psalms (*meditatio psalmorum*) has edified the saints for thousands of years and should be a regular part of our spiritual diet. It is enormously beneficial in all seasons and conditions of life to savor and absorb the meaning of the Psalms in the depths of one's heart.
- Ideally, meditation should address the mind, the emotions, and the will. Ruminating on Scripture stimulates our thinking and understanding and it also elevates the affections of the heart. It reaches the will when we resolve to let the passage shape our actions. Intellect, imagination, and volition should not be divorced from one another.
- Accept the fact that you will often encounter problems with distraction and inattention. Do not be disturbed when your mind wanders, but gently and calmly return to the text before you. As Thomas Merton stated in *New Seeds of Contemplation,* "It is much better to desire God without being able to think clearly of Him, than to have marvelous thoughts about Him without desiring to enter into union with His will." Normally, it is best to resist the temptation to be distracted by practical concerns, but sometimes it can be helpful to turn these concerns into subjects of meditation in light of the truth of the text.
- Remember that meditation does not need to produce evident affection or consolation in order to be beneficial. The quest for moving experiences can lead to the self-deception of emotional melodrama and counterfeit mysticism.

PRAYER (ORATIO)

The discipline of prayer is usually associated with a personal dialogue (colloquy) with God, though the majority of our prayers appear to be petitionary monologues. In *lectio divina,* prayer is specifically related to the two prior movements of sacred reading and meditation on the text. *Oratio* is the fruit of *meditatio,* and it is the way we "interiorize" what God has spoken to us through the passage. The transition from meditation to prayer may be subtle or unnoticed, but it is a response of the heart to what has been largely occupying the mind. It is a movement from truth to implication, from hearing to acknowledgment, from understanding to obedience.

Depending on how the "living and active" Word is shaping us (Hebrews 4:12), this period of prayer can be sweet and consoling, or it can be painful and revealing. The two-edged sword of the Spirit has a way of exposing the thoughts and intentions of the heart, and when our selfish, distorted, and manipulative strategies are "open and laid bare to the eyes of Him with whom we have to do" (Hebrews 4:13), *oratio* becomes a time for compunction, confession, and repentance. When the soul is exposed and we see our interior and exterior lives as God sees them, it can be both devastating (in light of God's holiness) and exhilarating (in light of God's forgiveness and compassion). At other times, we may be gripped by the power of spiritual truth (for example, the kindness and love of the Father, the grace and faithfulness of the Son, the fellowship and presence of the Spirit) and respond in adoration or thanksgiving. *Oratio* is a time for participation in the interpenetrating subjectivity of the Trinity through prolonged mutual presence and growing identification with the life of Christ.

Suggestions for Prayer

- Allow enough time so that you do not rush the process; you are not likely to listen to God when you are in a hurry.
- Avoid the rut of reducing this period of prayer to a technique or a routine.
- In *lectio divina*, there is a temptation to substitute reading for prayer. It is helpful to view your reading and meditation on the text as preparation for a personal, prayerful response.
- Do not seek to control the content or outcome of your prayer.
- Remember that *oratio* is a time for heart response as you move from the mind to the will. Prayer embraces the practical consequences of the truth you have seen and endeavors to direct your life in accordance with it.
- Depending on your reading and meditation, your response can take a number of different forms, including adoration, confession, renewal, petition, intercession, affirmation, and thanksgiving. All of these are different ways of calling upon the Lord, but at one time a prayer of adoration may be appropriate, while at another time the Spirit may lead you in a prayer of confession or petition.
- When the Lord speaks to you in the text by way of exhortation or encouragement, it is good to "pray it through" — that is, to take the time to internalize the message.
- See this time as an opportunity to move away from your false self (the flesh) toward your true self in Christ.
- Scripture is God-breathed and "profitable for teaching, for reproof, for correction, for training in righteousness" (2 Timothy 3:16). Invite the Spirit to search, teach, encourage, comfort, and correct you. Let Him reveal and dispel your illusions, pride, self-centeredness, stubbornness, ungodly attitudes and habits, stinginess, lack of gratitude, manipulation and control, and so forth.
- Prayer can occur at any time during the *lectio* process, and you may find yourself alternating between reading, meditation, and prayer. *Lectio divina* is not a lock-step, sequential movement.
- When you are distracted, simply return to the text to refocus your attention. Teresa of Avila used an image of prayer as a small fire that occasionally needs to be fed by adding a twig or two. A twig is a few words from Scripture, but too many words become branches that could extinguish the fire.
- Bear in mind that in *lectio divina*, prayer is part of the path that leads to contemplation.

CONTEMPLATION (CONTEMPLATIO)

Some who use the term *lectio divina* limit it primarily to slow, careful, and prayerful reading of a biblical passage, book, or other spiritual text rather than the whole movement from reading to meditation to prayer to contemplation. As I see it, however, the process of *lectio divina* should begin with reading and culminate in contemplation. Contemplation is often confused with meditation, but as we will see, they are not synonymous.

Meditation and the prayer that flows out of it bring us into communication with the living and transcendent Lord, and as such, they prepare us for contemplation. Meditative prayer should be more than an intellectual exercise; when it is accompanied by affective intention it leads to the love and communion of contemplative prayer. Because of its very nature, it is notoriously difficult to communicate the characteristics of contemplative prayer. It is a mysterious territory in which the language is silence and the action is receptivity. True contemplation is a theological grace that cannot be reduced to logical, psychological, or aesthetic categories. Perhaps these general contrasts between meditative and contemplative prayer will help:

MEDITATIVE PRAYER	CONTEMPLATIVE PRAYER
Speech	Silence
Activity	Receptivity
Discursive thought	Loss of mental images and concepts
Vocal and mental prayer	Wordless prayer and interior stillness
Natural faculties of reason and imagination	Mysterious darkening of the natural faculties
Affective feelings	Loss of feelings
Reading and reflection	Inability to meditate
Doing	Being
Seeking	Receiving
Talking to Jesus	Entering into the prayer of Jesus

When he witnessed the miracle of the transfiguration of Jesus on the holy mountain, the awe-struck Peter inappropriately broke into speech and was silenced by the voice out of the cloud that said, "This is My beloved Son, with whom I am well-pleased; listen to Him!" (Matthew 17:4-5). When we enter into the numinous territory of contemplation, it is best for us to stop talking and "listen to Him" in simple and loving attentiveness. In this strange and holy land we must remove the sandals of our ideas, constructs, and inclinations, and quietly listen for the voice of God. Periods of contemplation can be little "dark nights of faith." During these times, God may seem absent and silent, but His presence and speech is on a deeper level than what we can feel or understand. By preparing a peaceful place in the soul we learn to "rest in the Lord and wait patiently for Him" (Psalm 37:7).

A number of people have been exposed to aspects of contemplative prayer through *centering prayer,* a practice that was recently revived and updated by three Cistercian monks—Thomas Keating, William Meninger, and Basil Pennington. This method of prayer is based on the fourteenth-century classic of mystical theology, *The Cloud of Unknowing.* Another approach to contemplative prayer is the *prayer of the heart* that is described in the *Philokalia,* an anthology of quotations from Eastern monastic Fathers from the third century to the Middle Ages. In this tradition, the invocation of the name of the Lord Jesus is used to create a state of receptivity and interior recollection of the presence of God.

Suggestions for Contemplation

- Take enough time to present yourself before God in silence and yield-edness. Contemplative prayer involves the development of a deeper and more intuitive form of receptivity to the supernatural.
- As with meditation and prayer, do not be concerned with results, feelings, or experiences during contemplation. The important thing is to "appear before God" in a quiet and receptive mode of being.
- It is helpful to think of a word or an image that expresses what I call the *spirit of the passage* that you have been processing in your reading, meditation, and prayer. When your mind wanders during your time for contemplation, center yourself by returning once again to the spirit of the passage.
- Contemplation is a gift very few believers have attempted to develop. Expect that growth in this new terrain will involve time, discipline, and the frustration of apparent failure. Don't allow distractions or lack of initial benefits to dissuade you from this time-tested discipline. True contemplation may require years of fidelity, but any consistency in this practice will greatly reward you.
- Contemplation is especially difficult for more extroverted and sensory temperaments. This is a discipline of silence, of loss of control, of abandoning the attempt to analyze and intellectualize, and of developing the intuitive faculties.
- Remember that you cannot engage in contemplative prayer by your own effort; it is God's work, and it requires a *receptive passivity.* In contemplation it is best to abandon self-consciousness and to allow yourself to be drawn into the inexpressible depths of God's love
- Since *lectio divina* is not a rigid movement through four steps, you may find yourself going back to reading, meditation, or prayer and returning again to the interior silence of contemplation. The amount of time you spend in each of these four elements is up to you, and you should experiment with this. However, I recommend that you practice all four

since each of them has a unique benefit.

- Nourish your interior life by reducing your exposure to radio, television, and other forms of distraction and commotion.

My colleague George Grove uses the following set of analogies to integrate the four components of sacred reading:

LECTIO	MEDITATIO	ORATIO	CONTEMPLATIO
Read	Meditate	Pray	Abide
Lips	Mind	Heart	Spirit
Seek	Find	Knock	Open
Food	Chew	Savor	Fill

Lectio divina engages the whole person from the physical to the psychological to the inward spiritual center of our being. It promotes a harmonious unity through an organic process that uses a variety of means. Fidelity and consistency in this long-term activity will gradually enhance and enrich your life.

Suggestions for Sacred Reading as a Whole

- Do not reduce sacred reading to a technique, system, or program. It has been called a *methodless method* that contributes to the development of a mode of being toward God. It is a personal process that cultivates a spiritual outlook of trust, receptivity, expectation, worship, and intimacy with God.
- Always see yourself as a beginner in the sense that you never "master" this process. There is always more than we think. Remember that discipline and devotion reinforce each other.
- Feel free to adapt this spiritual formation approach to your temperament. More extroverted people, for example, will only be comfortable with short sessions, while more introverted people will tend to take more time in this process.
- Perhaps the most important suggestion I can make is for you to write out the verse or verses you have used for sacred reading on a given day and carry this card with you through your activities. By doing this, you are making that day's passage your theme for twenty-four hours and using it as a tool to practice the presence of Christ. These cards can also assist you in memorization by moving the texts from short-term to longer-term memory.
- It is possible for some personality types to develop a false supernaturalism by becoming immersed in an artificial experience. Thinking they are communing with God, they are really lost in themselves. This problem of self-delusion and misguided zeal can be corrected by a

willingness to accept sound advice through spiritual direction.

- To aspire to contemplation without cultivating compassion for others is to miss the point and purpose of contemplative prayer. The byproduct of devotional spirituality should always be an increased capacity to love and serve others. By the same token, a growing realization of our union with others in Christ will enhance our capacity to know God.

A BLEND OF CONTEMPLATION AND ACTION

The polarity between the contemplative life and the active life has been a source of tension for many centuries. Saint Gregory advocated a more contemplative approach to prayer as rest from exterior action in the quest for communion with God. Saint Basil promoted a more active approach to prayer in association with work. Carried too far, the contemplative extreme could divorce our primary calling to know God from our secondary calling to express this knowledge in the world. On the other hand, the active extreme tends to elevate our secondary calling of work to the point of replacing our primary calling. A more balanced approach integrates and honors both callings and unites the contemplative and active vocations. Saint Benedict encouraged this blended rhythm of rest and action, interior aspiration and exterior obedience, devotion and discipline, prayer and labor, desire for God and service of neighbor, the spring of living water and the stream that flows out of it. By uniting the strengths of both Mary and Martha, we can learn to be contemplatives in action.

CULTIVATING A PASSION FOR CHRIST

Devotional spirituality is like a delicate grapevine that flourishes only when it is planted in the right soil and carefully cultivated in a good climate. Unless it is nurtured, it will wither from neglect and fail to bear fruit. The fruit of spiritual passion can be threatened by natural enemies, but it can also be stimulated by several sources.

Enemies of Spiritual Passion

- *Unresolved areas of disobedience.* Resisting the prodding of God in an area of your life may seem subtle, but it can be a more serious grievance to the heart of God than we suppose. It is good to invite the Holy Spirit to reveal any barriers in our relationship with God or people that have been erected by sinful attitudes and actions. When these become evident, deal with them quickly and trust in the power of God's forgiveness through the blood of Christ.
- *Complacency.* Without holy desire we will succumb to the sin of spiritual *acedia:* indifference, apathy, and boredom. People who lose the sharp edge of intention and calling can slip into a morass of listlessness and feelings of failure. We must often ask God for the grace of

acute desire so that we will hunger and thirst for Him.

- *Erosion in spiritual disciplines.* Complacency can cause or be caused by a failure to train and remain disciplined in the spiritual life. There are several biblical figures like King Asa (2 Chronicles 14–16) who illustrate the problem of starting well in the first half of life and finishing poorly in the last half. When spiritual disciplines begin to erode, spiritual passion declines as well.
- *External obedience.* There are many people who are more concerned about conformity to rules, moral behavior, and duty than they are about loving Jesus. External obedience without inward affection falls short of the biblical vision of obeying God from the heart (Jeremiah 31:33; Romans 6:17; Ephesians 6:6).
- *Loving truth more than Christ.* Some students of the Word have come to love the content of truth in the Bible more than the Source of that truth. Biblical and systematic theology are worthy of pursuit, but not when they become substitutes for the pursuit of knowing and becoming like Jesus.
- *Elevating service and ministry above Christ.* It is easier to define ourselves by what we accomplish than by our new identity in Christ. For some, the Christian life consists more of fellowship, service to those in need, witnessing, and worship than of becoming intimate with Jesus. This leads to the problem of ministry without the manifest presence of God.
- *Greater commitment to institutions than to Christ.* It is easy for churches, denominations, or other organizations to occupy more of our time and attention than devotion to Jesus. There is a constant danger of getting more passionate about causes than about Christ.
- *A merely functional relationship.* Many people are more interested in what Jesus can do for them than in who He is. We may initially come to Him hoping that He will help us with our career, marriage, children, or health, but if we do not grow beyond this "gifts above the Giver" mentality, we will never develop spiritual passion.

Sources of Spiritual Passion

- *Growing awareness of God as a Person.* God is an intensely personal and relational Being, and it is an insult for us to treat Him as though He were a power or a principle. Some of us find it easier to be comfortable with abstract principles and ideas than with people and intimacy. As we have seen, good things like the Bible, theology, ministry, and church can become substitutes for loving Him. As a countermeasure, it is good to ask God for the grace of increased passion for His Son so that, by the power of the Spirit, we will come to love Him as the Father loves Him.
- *Sitting at Jesus' feet.* When we make consistent time for reading, meditation, prayer, and contemplation, we place ourselves at the feet of Jesus and enjoy His presence. By making ourselves available and receptive to

Him, we learn the wisdom of spending more time being a friend of Jesus than a friend of others.

- *Imitating the Master.* Our identification with Jesus in His death, burial, resurrection, and ascension has made us new creatures before God (2 Corinthians 5:17). This divinely- wrought identification makes it possible for us to imitate Jesus and "follow in His steps" (1 Peter 2:21). If we love the Master, we will want to be like Him in His character, humility, compassion, love, joy, peace, and dependence on the Father's will.

- *Cultivating spiritual affections.* Regardless of our natural temperaments, it is important for us to develop true affections (desire, longing, zeal, craving, hunger) for God. The rich emotional life of the psalmists (see Psalm 27:4; 42:1-3; 63:1-8; 145:1-21) reveals a desire for God above all else and a willingness to cling to Him during times of aridity and dryness. Like them, we must aspire to a love that is beyond us (Ephesians 3:17-19).

- *Increasing appreciation for the goodness of God.* The distractions of the world make it difficult for us to develop a growing appreciation for our relationship with God. We forget that we can enjoy communion with Someone who is infinitely better than the objects of our most powerful natural desires. We must pray for the grace of gratitude and amazement at the unqualified goodness of God's "kindness toward us in Christ Jesus" (Ephesians 2:7).

- *Focused intention.* What do you want (or want to want) more than anything else? God is pleased when we pursue Him with a heart that is intent on knowing and loving Him. He "begins His influence by working in us that we may have the will, and He completes it by working with us when we have the will" (Augustine, *On Grace and Free Will*). As our wills become more simplified and centered on becoming like Jesus, our love for Him will grow.

- *Willingness to let God break the outward self.* "Unless a grain of wheat falls into the earth and dies, it remains alone; but if it dies, it bears much fruit. He who loves his life loses it, and he who hates his life in this world will keep it to life eternal" (John 12:24-25). The alabaster vial of the self-life must be broken (Mark 14:3) to release the perfume of the new self in Christ. If we wish to manifest the fragrance of Christ, we must allow God to bring us (in His time and way) to the painful place of brokenness on the cross of self-abandonment to Him. This theme resonates in spiritual literature, and one of the clearest expressions is in Watchman Nee's *The Release of the Spirit*.

- *Desiring to please God more than to impress people.* If we want to be like Christ, we must embrace His governing goal to be pleasing to the Father (John 8:29; Hebrews 10:7). The enemy of this glorious goal is the competing quest for human approval (John 5:41, 44; 12:43; Galatians 1:10). We cannot have it both ways; we will either play to an

Audience of One or to an audience of many. But in the end, only God's opinion will matter.

- *Treasuring God.* Dallas Willard observes in *The Divine Conspiracy* that God "treasures those whom he has created, planned for, longed for, sorrowed over, redeemed, and befriended." Just as God has treasured us, so He wants us to respond by treasuring Him above all else. "We love, because He first loved us" (1 John 4:19)—the more we realize how God loved and valued us, the greater our capacity to love and value Him. In *Beginning to Pray,* Anthony Bloom suggests that one way to treasure God is to find a personal name or expression for God that flows out of our relationship with Him, like David's "You, my Joy!"

- *Maturing in trust.* As believers, we trust Christ for our eternal destiny, but most of us find it difficult to trust Him in our daily practice. As long as we pursue sinful strategies of seeking satisfaction on our own terms, our confidence will be misplaced. We must learn to trust Jesus enough to place our confidence in His power, not in our performance.

GETTING THE MOST OUT OF THIS JOURNAL

This is one of four journals in the *Reflections* series, and it is designed to guide you through three months of *lectio divina* passages. I have selected ninety texts from Numbers through Revelation that are particularly well-suited to the process of sacred reading. These texts range from one to several verses, and they are arranged in biblical sequence to attune you to the flow of progressive revelation. I have translated the verses from the original languages, and in several cases I have adapted and personalized them.

The daily four-part sequence of reading, meditation, prayer, and contemplation invites you to engage personally with the text and to record your thoughts and prayers in the process. This journaling component will enhance your interaction with each of the readings, and it will yield a valuable record of your reflections and prayers during these months. When you have completed this journal of sacred readings, you will profit from reading through the comments and prayers you have recorded.

I also suggest you go through this process a second time and visit each of these passages once again. You will discover new things in the Scripture texts that you did not see the first time through.

> *May the God of our Lord Jesus Christ, the Father of glory, give*
> *you a spirit of wisdom and of revelation in the full knowledge of*
> *Him, and may the eyes of your heart be enlightened, in order that*
> *you may know what is the hope of His calling, what are the*
> *riches of His glorious inheritance in the saints, and what is the*
> *incomparable greatness of His power toward us who believe.*
>
> —Ephesians 1:17-19

O my soul, above all things and in all things always rest in the Lord, for He is the eternal rest of the saints.

Grant me most sweet and loving Jesus, to rest in You above every other creature, above all health and beauty, above all glory and honor, above all power and dignity, above all knowledge and precise thought, above all wealth and talent, above all joy and exultation, above all fame and praise, above all sweetness and consolation, above all hope and promise, above all merit and desire, above all gifts and favors You give and shower upon me, above all happiness and joy that the mind can understand and feel, and finally, above all angels and archangels, above all the hosts of heaven, above all things visible and invisible, and above all that is not You, my God.

—Thomas à Kempis, *The Imitation of Christ*

SCRIPTURE

The Lord bless you and keep you;
The Lord make His face shine upon you
And be gracious to you;
The Lord turn His face toward you
And give you peace. (Numbers 6:24-26)

READING

Slowly read the Scripture passage several times.

MEDITATION

Take some time to reflect on the words and phrases in the text.
Which words, phrases, or images speak most to you?

PRAYER

Offer the internalized passage back to God in the form of a personalized
prayer of adoration, confession, renewal, petition, intercession,
affirmation, or thanksgiving.

CONTEMPLATION

What word or image captures the spirit of the passage for you?

Take a few minutes to present yourself before God in silence and
yieldedness. When your mind wanders, center yourself by returning to
the spirit of the passage.

S CRIPTURE

This book of the law will not depart from your mouth, but you will meditate on it day and night, so that you may be careful to do according to all that is written in it; for then you will make your way prosperous, and you will act wisely. (Joshua 1:8)

R EADING

Slowly read the Scripture passage several times.

M EDITATION

Take some time to reflect on the words and phrases in the text.
Which words, phrases, or images speak most to you?

P RAYER

Offer the internalized passage back to God in the form of a personalized prayer of adoration, confession, renewal, petition, intercession, affirmation, or thanksgiving.

C ONTEMPLATION

What word or image captures the spirit of the passage for you?

Take a few minutes to present yourself before God in silence and yieldedness. When your mind wanders, center yourself by returning to the spirit of the passage.

SCRIPTURE

As for God, His way is perfect;
The word of the Lord is proven.
He is a shield for all who take refuge in Him.
For who is God besides the Lord?
And who is the Rock except our God? (2 Samuel 22:31-32)

READING

Slowly read the Scripture passage several times.

MEDITATION

Take some time to reflect on the words and phrases in the text.
Which words, phrases, or images speak most to you?

PRAYER

Offer the internalized passage back to God in the form of a personalized
prayer of adoration, confession, renewal, petition, intercession,
affirmation, or thanksgiving.

CONTEMPLATION

What word or image captures the spirit of the passage for you?

Take a few minutes to present yourself before God in silence and
yieldedness. When your mind wanders, center yourself by returning to
the spirit of the passage.

SCRIPTURE

The Lord is great and greatly to be praised;
He is to be feared above all gods.
For all the gods of the nations are idols,
But the Lord made the heavens.
Splendor and majesty are before Him;
Strength and joy are in His place.
Ascribe to the Lord, O families of the nations,
Ascribe to the Lord glory and strength.
Ascribe to the Lord the glory due His name;
Bring an offering, and come before Him.
Worship the Lord in the beauty of holiness.
Tremble before Him, all the earth.
The world is firmly established; it will not be moved.
(1 Chronicles 16:25-30)

READING

Slowly read the Scripture passage several times.

MEDITATION

Take some time to reflect on the words and phrases in the text.
Which words, phrases, or images speak most to you?

PRAYER

Offer the internalized passage back to God in the form of a personalized prayer of adoration, confession, renewal, petition, intercession, affirmation, or thanksgiving.

CONTEMPLATION

What word or image captures the spirit of the passage for you?

Take a few minutes to present yourself before God in silence and yieldedness. When your mind wanders, center yourself by returning to the spirit of the passage.

SCRIPTURE

May I know God and serve Him with a whole heart and with a willing mind; for the Lord searches all hearts and understands every motive behind the thoughts. (1 Chronicles 28:9)

READING

Slowly read the Scripture passage several times.

MEDITATION

Take some time to reflect on the words and phrases in the text. Which words, phrases, or images speak most to you?

PRAYER

Offer the internalized passage back to God in the form of a personalized prayer of adoration, confession, renewal, petition, intercession, affirmation, or thanksgiving.

CONTEMPLATION

What word or image captures the spirit of the passage for you?

Take a few minutes to present yourself before God in silence and yieldedness. When your mind wanders, center yourself by returning to the spirit of the passage.

SCRIPTURE

You alone are the Lord.
You made the heavens,
The heaven of heavens, and all their host,
The earth and all that is on it,
The seas and all that is in them.
You give life to all that is in them,
And the host of heaven worships You. (Nehemiah 9:6)

READING

Slowly read the Scripture passage several times.

MEDITATION

Take some time to reflect on the words and phrases in the text.
Which words, phrases, or images speak most to you?

PRAYER

Offer the internalized passage back to God in the form of a personalized
prayer of adoration, confession, renewal, petition, intercession,
affirmation, or thanksgiving.

CONTEMPLATION

What word or image captures the spirit of the passage for you?

Take a few minutes to present yourself before God in silence and
yieldedness. When your mind wanders, center yourself by returning to
the spirit of the passage.

SCRIPTURE

Naked I came from my mother's womb,
And naked I will depart.
The Lord gives, and the Lord takes away;
Blessed be the name of the Lord. (Job 1:21)

READING

Slowly read the Scripture passage several times.

MEDITATION

Take some time to reflect on the words and phrases in the text.
Which words, phrases, or images speak most to you?

PRAYER

Offer the internalized passage back to God in the form of a personalized
prayer of adoration, confession, renewal, petition, intercession,
affirmation, or thanksgiving.

CONTEMPLATION

What word or image captures the spirit of the passage for you?

Take a few minutes to present yourself before God in silence and
yieldedness. When your mind wanders, center yourself by returning to
the spirit of the passage.

SCRIPTURE

Blessed is the man who does not walk in the counsel of the wicked
Or stand in the way of sinners
Or sit in the seat of scorners.
But his delight is in the law of the Lord,
And on His law he meditates day and night.
And he shall be like a tree planted by streams of water,
Which yields its fruit in its season
And whose leaf does not wither;
And whatever he does will prosper. (Psalm 1:1-3)

READING

Slowly read the Scripture passage several times.

MEDITATION

Take some time to reflect on the words and phrases in the text.
Which words, phrases, or images speak most to you?

PRAYER

Offer the internalized passage back to God in the form of a personalized prayer of adoration, confession, renewal, petition, intercession, affirmation, or thanksgiving.

CONTEMPLATION

What word or image captures the spirit of the passage for you?

Take a few minutes to present yourself before God in silence and yieldedness. When your mind wanders, center yourself by returning to the spirit of the passage.

SCRIPTURE

I love You, O Lord, my strength.
The Lord is my rock and my fortress and my deliverer;
My God is my rock, in whom I take refuge.
He is my shield and the horn of my salvation, my stronghold.
I call upon the Lord, who is worthy of praise,
And I am saved from my enemies. (Psalm 18:1-3)

READING

Slowly read the Scripture passage several times.

MEDITATION

Take some time to reflect on the words and phrases in the text.
Which words, phrases, or images speak most to you?

PRAYER

Offer the internalized passage back to God in the form of a personalized
prayer of adoration, confession, renewal, petition, intercession,
affirmation, or thanksgiving.

CONTEMPLATION

What word or image captures the spirit of the passage for you?

Take a few minutes to present yourself before God in silence and
yieldedness. When your mind wanders, center yourself by returning to
the spirit of the passage.

SCRIPTURE

The law of the Lord is perfect, restoring the soul.
The testimony of the Lord is sure, making wise the simple.
The precepts of the Lord are right, rejoicing the heart.
The commandment of the Lord is pure, enlightening the eyes.
The fear of the Lord is clean, enduring forever.
The judgments of the Lord are true and altogether righteous.
They are more desirable than gold, than much pure gold;
They are sweeter than honey, than honey from the comb.
Moreover, by them is Your servant warned;
In keeping them there is great reward. (Psalm 19:7-11)

READING

Slowly read the Scripture passage several times.

MEDITATION

Take some time to reflect on the words and phrases in the text.
Which words, phrases, or images speak most to you?

PRAYER

Offer the internalized passage back to God in the form of a personalized
prayer of adoration, confession, renewal, petition, intercession,
affirmation, or thanksgiving.

CONTEMPLATION

What word or image captures the spirit of the passage for you?

Take a few minutes to present yourself before God in silence and
yieldedness. When your mind wanders, center yourself by returning to
the spirit of the passage.

SCRIPTURE

How great is Your goodness,
Which You have stored up for those who fear You,
Which You have prepared for those who take refuge in You
Before the sons of men! (Psalm 31:19)

READING

Slowly read the Scripture passage several times.

MEDITATION

Take some time to reflect on the words and phrases in the text.
Which words, phrases, or images speak most to you?

PRAYER

Offer the internalized passage back to God in the form of a personalized
prayer of adoration, confession, renewal, petition, intercession,
affirmation, or thanksgiving.

CONTEMPLATION

What word or image captures the spirit of the passage for you?

Take a few minutes to present yourself before God in silence and
yieldedness. When your mind wanders, center yourself by returning to
the spirit of the passage.

SCRIPTURE

You are my hiding place;
You will preserve me from trouble
And surround me with songs of deliverance.
You will instruct me and teach me in the way I should go;
You will counsel me and watch over me. (Psalm 32:7-8)

READING

Slowly read the Scripture passage several times.

MEDITATION

Take some time to reflect on the words and phrases in the text.
Which words, phrases, or images speak most to you?

PRAYER

Offer the internalized passage back to God in the form of a personalized prayer of adoration, confession, renewal, petition, intercession, affirmation, or thanksgiving.

CONTEMPLATION

What word or image captures the spirit of the passage for you?

Take a few minutes to present yourself before God in silence and yieldedness. When your mind wanders, center yourself by returning to the spirit of the passage.

SCRIPTURE

May I trust in the Lord and do good; may I dwell in the land and feed on His faithfulness. When I delight myself in the Lord, He will give me the desires of my heart. I will commit my way to the Lord and trust in Him, and He will bring it to pass. He will bring forth my righteousness like the light, and my justice like the noonday. May I rest in the Lord and wait patiently for Him; I will not fret because of him who prospers in his way, because of the man who practices evil schemes. (Psalm 37:3-7)

READING

Slowly read the Scripture passage several times.

MEDITATION

Take some time to reflect on the words and phrases in the text.
Which words, phrases, or images speak most to you?

PRAYER

Offer the internalized passage back to God in the form of a personalized prayer of adoration, confession, renewal, petition, intercession, affirmation, or thanksgiving.

CONTEMPLATION

What word or image captures the spirit of the passage for you?

Take a few minutes to present yourself before God in silence and yieldedness. When your mind wanders, center yourself by returning to the spirit of the passage.

SCRIPTURE

As the deer pants for the water brooks,
So my soul pants for You, O God.
My soul thirsts for God, for the living God.
When shall I come and appear before God? (Psalm 42:1-2)

READING

Slowly read the Scripture passage several times.

MEDITATION

Take some time to reflect on the words and phrases in the text.
Which words, phrases, or images speak most to you?

PRAYER

Offer the internalized passage back to God in the form of a personalized
prayer of adoration, confession, renewal, petition, intercession,
affirmation, or thanksgiving.

CONTEMPLATION

What word or image captures the spirit of the passage for you?

Take a few minutes to present yourself before God in silence and
yieldedness. When your mind wanders, center yourself by returning to
the spirit of the passage.

SCRIPTURE

Whom have I in heaven but You?
And there is nothing on earth I desire besides You.
My flesh and my heart may fail,
But God is the strength of my heart and my portion forever.
Those who are far from You will perish;
You have cut off all who are unfaithful to You.
But as for me, the nearness of God is my good.
I have made the Lord God my refuge,
That I may tell of all Your works. (Psalm 73:25-28)

READING

Slowly read the Scripture passage several times.

MEDITATION

Take some time to reflect on the words and phrases in the text.
Which words, phrases, or images speak most to you?

PRAYER

Offer the internalized passage back to God in the form of a personalized prayer of adoration, confession, renewal, petition, intercession, affirmation, or thanksgiving.

CONTEMPLATION

What word or image captures the spirit of the passage for you?

Take a few minutes to present yourself before God in silence and yieldedness. When your mind wanders, center yourself by returning to the spirit of the passage.

SCRIPTURE

How great are Your works, O Lord!
Your thoughts are very deep.
The senseless man does not know;
Fools do not understand
That when the wicked spring up like grass
And all the evildoers flourish,
They will be destroyed forever.
But You, O Lord, are exalted forever. (Psalm 92:5-8)

READING

Slowly read the Scripture passage several times.

MEDITATION

Take some time to reflect on the words and phrases in the text.
Which words, phrases, or images speak most to you?

PRAYER

Offer the internalized passage back to God in the form of a personalized
prayer of adoration, confession, renewal, petition, intercession,
affirmation, or thanksgiving.

CONTEMPLATION

What word or image captures the spirit of the passage for you?

Take a few minutes to present yourself before God in silence and
yieldedness. When your mind wanders, center yourself by returning to
the spirit of the passage.

SCRIPTURE

God will not always strive with us,
Nor will He harbor His anger forever;
He does not treat us as our sins deserve
Or repay us according to our iniquities.
For as high as the heavens are above the earth,
So great is His love for those who fear Him;
As far as the east is from the west,
So far has He removed our transgressions from us.
As a father has compassion on his children,
So the Lord has compassion on those who fear Him. (Psalm 103:9-13)

READING

Slowly read the Scripture passage several times.

MEDITATION

Take some time to reflect on the words and phrases in the text.
Which words, phrases, or images speak most to you?

PRAYER

Offer the internalized passage back to God in the form of a personalized prayer of adoration, confession, renewal, petition, intercession, affirmation, or thanksgiving.

CONTEMPLATION

What word or image captures the spirit of the passage for you?

Take a few minutes to present yourself before God in silence and yieldedness. When your mind wanders, center yourself by returning to the spirit of the passage.

SCRIPTURE

You know how I am formed;
You remember that I am dust.
As for man, his days are like grass;
He flourishes like a flower of the field.
The wind passes over it and it is gone,
And its place remembers it no more.
But the lovingkindness of the Lord is from everlasting to everlasting
On those who fear Him,
And His righteousness with their children's children,
To those who keep His covenant
And remember to obey His precepts. (Psalm 103:14-18)

READING

Slowly read the Scripture passage several times.

MEDITATION

Take some time to reflect on the words and phrases in the text.
Which words, phrases, or images speak most to you?

PRAYER

Offer the internalized passage back to God in the form of a personalized
prayer of adoration, confession, renewal, petition, intercession,
affirmation, or thanksgiving.

CONTEMPLATION

What word or image captures the spirit of the passage for you?

Take a few minutes to present yourself before God in silence and
yieldedness. When your mind wanders, center yourself by returning to
the spirit of the passage.

SCRIPTURE

I will meditate on Your precepts
And consider Your ways.
I will delight in Your statutes,
And not forget Your word.
Deal bountifully with Your servant,
That I may live and keep Your word.
Open my eyes that I may see
Wonderful things from Your law. (Psalm 119:15-18)

READING

Slowly read the Scripture passage several times.

MEDITATION

Take some time to reflect on the words and phrases in the text.
Which words, phrases, or images speak most to you?

PRAYER

Offer the internalized passage back to God in the form of a personalized
prayer of adoration, confession, renewal, petition, intercession,
affirmation, or thanksgiving.

CONTEMPLATION

What word or image captures the spirit of the passage for you?

Take a few minutes to present yourself before God in silence and
yieldedness. When your mind wanders, center yourself by returning to
the spirit of the passage.

SCRIPTURE

The fear of the Lord is the beginning of knowledge,
But fools despise wisdom and discipline.
The fear of the Lord is a fountain of life,
To turn one away from the snares of death.
The secret of the Lord is with those who fear Him,
And He will make them know His covenant.
(Proverbs 1:7; 14:27; Psalm 25:14)

READING

Slowly read the Scripture passage several times.

MEDITATION

Take some time to reflect on the words and phrases in the text.
Which words, phrases, or images speak most to you?

PRAYER

Offer the internalized passage back to God in the form of a personalized
prayer of adoration, confession, renewal, petition, intercession,
affirmation, or thanksgiving.

CONTEMPLATION

What word or image captures the spirit of the passage for you?

Take a few minutes to present yourself before God in silence and
yieldedness. When your mind wanders, center yourself by returning to
the spirit of the passage.

SCRIPTURE

Trust in the Lord with all your heart
And not do not lean on your own understanding;
In all your ways acknowledge Him,
And He will make your paths straight.
Do not be wise in your own eyes,
But fear the Lord and depart from evil. (Proverbs 3:5-7)

READING

Slowly read the Scripture passage several times.

MEDITATION

Take some time to reflect on the words and phrases in the text.
Which words, phrases, or images speak most to you?

PRAYER

Offer the internalized passage back to God in the form of a personalized
prayer of adoration, confession, renewal, petition, intercession,
affirmation, or thanksgiving.

CONTEMPLATION

What word or image captures the spirit of the passage for you?

Take a few minutes to present yourself before God in silence and
yieldedness. When your mind wanders, center yourself by returning to
the spirit of the passage.

SCRIPTURE

In his heart a man plans his way,
But the Lord determines his steps.
Many are the plans in a person's heart,
But it is the counsel of the Lord that will stand.
There is no wisdom or understanding
Or counsel that can succeed against the Lord.
(Proverbs 16:9; 19:21; 21:30)

READING

Slowly read the Scripture passage several times.

MEDITATION

Take some time to reflect on the words and phrases in the text.
Which words, phrases, or images speak most to you?

PRAYER

Offer the internalized passage back to God in the form of a personalized
prayer of adoration, confession, renewal, petition, intercession,
affirmation, or thanksgiving.

CONTEMPLATION

What word or image captures the spirit of the passage for you?

Take a few minutes to present yourself before God in silence and
yieldedness. When your mind wanders, center yourself by returning to
the spirit of the passage.

SCRIPTURE

This is what the Lord God, the Holy One of Israel, says:
"In repentance and rest is your salvation;
In quietness and trust is your strength." (Isaiah 30:15)

READING

Slowly read the Scripture passage several times.

MEDITATION

Take some time to reflect on the words and phrases in the text.
Which words, phrases, or images speak most to you?

PRAYER

Offer the internalized passage back to God in the form of a personalized
prayer of adoration, confession, renewal, petition, intercession,
affirmation, or thanksgiving.

CONTEMPLATION

What word or image captures the spirit of the passage for you?

Take a few minutes to present yourself before God in silence and
yieldedness. When your mind wanders, center yourself by returning to
the spirit of the passage.

SCRIPTURE

You were pierced for our transgressions,
You were crushed for our iniquities;
The punishment that brought us peace was upon You,
And by Your wounds we are healed.
All of us like sheep have gone astray,
Each of us has turned to his own way,
And the Lord has laid on You the iniquity of us all. (Isaiah 53:5-6)

READING

Slowly read the Scripture passage several times.

MEDITATION

Take some time to reflect on the words and phrases in the text.
Which words, phrases, or images speak most to you?

PRAYER

Offer the internalized passage back to God in the form of a personalized
prayer of adoration, confession, renewal, petition, intercession,
affirmation, or thanksgiving.

CONTEMPLATION

What word or image captures the spirit of the passage for you?

Take a few minutes to present yourself before God in silence and
yieldedness. When your mind wanders, center yourself by returning to
the spirit of the passage.

SCRIPTURE

This is the one You esteem:
He who is humble and contrite of spirit,
And who trembles at Your word. (Isaiah 66:2b)

READING

Slowly read the Scripture passage several times.

MEDITATION

Take some time to reflect on the words and phrases in the text.
Which words, phrases, or images speak most to you?

PRAYER

Offer the internalized passage back to God in the form of a personalized
prayer of adoration, confession, renewal, petition, intercession,
affirmation, or thanksgiving.

CONTEMPLATION

What word or image captures the spirit of the passage for you?

Take a few minutes to present yourself before God in silence and
yieldedness. When your mind wanders, center yourself by returning to
the spirit of the passage.

SCRIPTURE

Thus says the Lord: "Let not the wise man boast of his wisdom, and let not the strong man boast of his strength, and let not the rich man boast of his riches; but let him who boasts boast about this: that he understands and knows Me, that I am the Lord, who exercises lovingkindness, justice, and righteousness on earth; for in these I delight," declares the Lord. (Jeremiah 9:23-24)

READING

Slowly read the Scripture passage several times.

MEDITATION

Take some time to reflect on the words and phrases in the text. Which words, phrases, or images speak most to you?

PRAYER

Offer the internalized passage back to God in the form of a personalized prayer of adoration, confession, renewal, petition, intercession, affirmation, or thanksgiving.

CONTEMPLATION

What word or image captures the spirit of the passage for you?

Take a few minutes to present yourself before God in silence and yieldedness. When your mind wanders, center yourself by returning to the spirit of the passage.

SCRIPTURE

Cursed is the one who trusts in man,
Who depends on flesh for his strength
And whose heart turns away from the Lord.
But blessed is the one who trusts in the Lord,
Whose confidence is in Him. (Jeremiah 17:5, 7)

READING

Slowly read the Scripture passage several times.

MEDITATION

Take some time to reflect on the words and phrases in the text.
Which words, phrases, or images speak most to you?

PRAYER

Offer the internalized passage back to God in the form of a personalized
prayer of adoration, confession, renewal, petition, intercession,
affirmation, or thanksgiving.

CONTEMPLATION

What word or image captures the spirit of the passage for you?

Take a few minutes to present yourself before God in silence and
yieldedness. When your mind wanders, center yourself by returning to
the spirit of the passage.

SCRIPTURE

"I know the plans I have for you," declares the Lord, "plans to prosper you and not to harm you, plans to give you a future and a hope."
(Jeremiah 29:11)

READING

Slowly read the Scripture passage several times.

MEDITATION

Take some time to reflect on the words and phrases in the text.
Which words, phrases, or images speak most to you?

PRAYER

Offer the internalized passage back to God in the form of a personalized prayer of adoration, confession, renewal, petition, intercession, affirmation, or thanksgiving.

CONTEMPLATION

What word or image captures the spirit of the passage for you?

Take a few minutes to present yourself before God in silence and yieldedness. When your mind wanders, center yourself by returning to the spirit of the passage.

SCRIPTURE

I call this to mind,
And therefore I have hope:
The Lord's mercies never cease,
For His compassions never fail.
They are new every morning;
Great is Your faithfulness. (Lamentations 3:21-23)

READING

Slowly read the Scripture passage several times.

MEDITATION

Take some time to reflect on the words and phrases in the text.
Which words, phrases, or images speak most to you?

PRAYER

Offer the internalized passage back to God in the form of a personalized
prayer of adoration, confession, renewal, petition, intercession,
affirmation, or thanksgiving.

CONTEMPLATION

What word or image captures the spirit of the passage for you?

Take a few minutes to present yourself before God in silence and
yieldedness. When your mind wanders, center yourself by returning to
the spirit of the passage.

SCRIPTURE

"The Lord is my portion," says my soul,
"Therefore I will wait for Him."
The Lord is good to those who wait for Him,
To the soul who seeks Him.
It is good to hope silently
For the salvation of the Lord. (Lamentations 3:24-26)

READING

Slowly read the Scripture passage several times.

MEDITATION

Take some time to reflect on the words and phrases in the text.
Which words, phrases, or images speak most to you?

PRAYER

Offer the internalized passage back to God in the form of a personalized prayer of adoration, confession, renewal, petition, intercession, affirmation, or thanksgiving.

CONTEMPLATION

What word or image captures the spirit of the passage for you?

Take a few minutes to present yourself before God in silence and yieldedness. When your mind wanders, center yourself by returning to the spirit of the passage.

SCRIPTURE

You have shown me what is good;
And what does the Lord require of me
But to act justly and to love mercy
And to walk humbly with my God? (Micah 6:8)

READING

Slowly read the Scripture passage several times.

MEDITATION

Take some time to reflect on the words and phrases in the text.
Which words, phrases, or images speak most to you?

PRAYER

Offer the internalized passage back to God in the form of a personalized
prayer of adoration, confession, renewal, petition, intercession,
affirmation, or thanksgiving.

CONTEMPLATION

What word or image captures the spirit of the passage for you?

Take a few minutes to present yourself before God in silence and
yieldedness. When your mind wanders, center yourself by returning to
the spirit of the passage.

SCRIPTURE

I will exult in the Lord;
I will rejoice in the God of my salvation.
The Lord God is my strength;
He makes my feet like the feet of a deer
And enables me to go on the heights. (Habakkuk 3:18-19)

READING

Slowly read the Scripture passage several times.

MEDITATION

Take some time to reflect on the words and phrases in the text.
Which words, phrases, or images speak most to you?

PRAYER

Offer the internalized passage back to God in the form of a personalized prayer of adoration, confession, renewal, petition, intercession, affirmation, or thanksgiving.

CONTEMPLATION

What word or image captures the spirit of the passage for you?

Take a few minutes to present yourself before God in silence and yieldedness. When your mind wanders, center yourself by returning to the spirit of the passage.

SCRIPTURE

"You are the salt of the earth, but if the salt loses its flavor, how can it be made salty again? It is no longer good for anything, except to be thrown out and trampled underfoot by men. You are the light of the world. A city set on a hill cannot be hidden. Neither do people light a lamp and put it under a basket, but on a lampstand, and it gives light to all who are in the house. Let your light shine before men, that they may see your good deeds and praise your Father in heaven." (Matthew 5:13-16)

READING

Slowly read the Scripture passage several times.

MEDITATION

Take some time to reflect on the words and phrases in the text.
Which words, phrases, or images speak most to you?

PRAYER

Offer the internalized passage back to God in the form of a personalized prayer of adoration, confession, renewal, petition, intercession, affirmation, or thanksgiving.

CONTEMPLATION

What word or image captures the spirit of the passage for you?

Take a few minutes to present yourself before God in silence and yieldedness. When your mind wanders, center yourself by returning to the spirit of the passage.

SCRIPTURE

"Come to Me, all you who labor and are heavy laden, and I will give you rest. Take My yoke upon you and learn from Me, for I am gentle and humble in heart, and you will find rest for your souls. For My yoke is easy, and My burden is light." (Matthew 11:28-30)

READING

Slowly read the Scripture passage several times.

MEDITATION

Take some time to reflect on the words and phrases in the text. Which words, phrases, or images speak most to you?

PRAYER

Offer the internalized passage back to God in the form of a personalized prayer of adoration, confession, renewal, petition, intercession, affirmation, or thanksgiving.

CONTEMPLATION

What word or image captures the spirit of the passage for you?

Take a few minutes to present yourself before God in silence and yieldedness. When your mind wanders, center yourself by returning to the spirit of the passage.

SCRIPTURE

"If anyone wishes to come after Me, he must deny himself and take up his cross and follow Me. For whoever wants to save his life will lose it, but whoever loses his life for My sake and the gospel's will find it. For what is a man profited if he gains the whole world, yet forfeits his soul? Or what will a man give in exchange for his soul?" (Matthew 16:24-26; Mark 8:34-37; Luke 9:23-25)

READING

Slowly read the Scripture passage several times.

MEDITATION

Take some time to reflect on the words and phrases in the text.
Which words, phrases, or images speak most to you?

PRAYER

Offer the internalized passage back to God in the form of a personalized prayer of adoration, confession, renewal, petition, intercession, affirmation, or thanksgiving.

CONTEMPLATION

What word or image captures the spirit of the passage for you?

Take a few minutes to present yourself before God in silence and yieldedness. When your mind wanders, center yourself by returning to the spirit of the passage.

SCRIPTURE

"All authority has been given to Me in heaven and on earth. Go therefore and make disciples of all nations, baptizing them in the name of the Father and of the Son and of the Holy Spirit, teaching them to observe everything I have commanded you. And surely I am with you always, even to the end of the age." (Matthew 28:18-20)

READING

Slowly read the Scripture passage several times.

MEDITATION

Take some time to reflect on the words and phrases in the text. Which words, phrases, or images speak most to you?

PRAYER

Offer the internalized passage back to God in the form of a personalized prayer of adoration, confession, renewal, petition, intercession, affirmation, or thanksgiving.

CONTEMPLATION

What word or image captures the spirit of the passage for you?

Take a few minutes to present yourself before God in silence and yieldedness. When your mind wanders, center yourself by returning to the spirit of the passage.

SCRIPTURE

My soul magnifies the Lord
And my spirit rejoices in God my Savior,
For the Mighty One has done great things for me,
And holy is His name.
His mercy is on those who fear Him,
From generation to generation. (Luke 1:46-47, 49-50)

READING

Slowly read the Scripture passage several times.

MEDITATION

Take some time to reflect on the words and phrases in the text.
Which words, phrases, or images speak most to you?

PRAYER

Offer the internalized passage back to God in the form of a personalized
prayer of adoration, confession, renewal, petition, intercession,
affirmation, or thanksgiving.

CONTEMPLATION

What word or image captures the spirit of the passage for you?

Take a few minutes to present yourself before God in silence and
yieldedness. When your mind wanders, center yourself by returning to
the spirit of the passage.

SCRIPTURE

*"He who is faithful with very little is also faithful with much, and who-
ever is dishonest with very little will also be dishonest with much. If one is
not faithful in handling worldly wealth, who will trust him with true
riches? And if one is not faithful with someone else's property, who will
give him property of his own?"* (Luke 16:10-12)

READING

Slowly read the Scripture passage several times.

MEDITATION

Take some time to reflect on the words and phrases in the text.
Which words, phrases, or images speak most to you?

PRAYER

Offer the internalized passage back to God in the form of a personalized
prayer of adoration, confession, renewal, petition, intercession,
affirmation, or thanksgiving.

CONTEMPLATION

What word or image captures the spirit of the passage for you?

Take a few minutes to present yourself before God in silence and
yieldedness. When your mind wanders, center yourself by returning to
the spirit of the passage.

SCRIPTURE

"Unless a grain of wheat falls to the ground and dies, it remains alone. But if it dies, it bears much fruit. The one who loves his life will lose it, and the one who hates his life in this world will keep it for eternal life." (John 12:24-25)

READING

Slowly read the Scripture passage several times.

MEDITATION

Take some time to reflect on the words and phrases in the text. Which words, phrases, or images speak most to you?

PRAYER

Offer the internalized passage back to God in the form of a personalized prayer of adoration, confession, renewal, petition, intercession, affirmation, or thanksgiving.

CONTEMPLATION

What word or image captures the spirit of the passage for you?

Take a few minutes to present yourself before God in silence and yieldedness. When your mind wanders, center yourself by returning to the spirit of the passage.

SCRIPTURE

"He who has My commandments and obeys them, he is the one who loves Me; and he who loves Me will be loved by My Father, and I will love him and reveal Myself to him." (John 14:21)

READING

Slowly read the Scripture passage several times.

MEDITATION

Take some time to reflect on the words and phrases in the text. Which words, phrases, or images speak most to you?

PRAYER

Offer the internalized passage back to God in the form of a personalized prayer of adoration, confession, renewal, petition, intercession, affirmation, or thanksgiving.

CONTEMPLATION

What word or image captures the spirit of the passage for you?

Take a few minutes to present yourself before God in silence and yieldedness. When your mind wanders, center yourself by returning to the spirit of the passage.

SCRIPTURE

"Peace I leave with you; My peace I give to you. Not as the world gives, do I give to you. Do not let your hearts be troubled, nor let them be afraid." (John 14:27)

READING

Slowly read the Scripture passage several times.

MEDITATION

Take some time to reflect on the words and phrases in the text. Which words, phrases, or images speak most to you?

PRAYER

Offer the internalized passage back to God in the form of a personalized prayer of adoration, confession, renewal, petition, intercession, affirmation, or thanksgiving.

CONTEMPLATION

What word or image captures the spirit of the passage for you?

Take a few minutes to present yourself before God in silence and yieldedness. When your mind wanders, center yourself by returning to the spirit of the passage.

SCRIPTURE

"I am the true vine, and My Father is the vinedresser. He cuts off every branch in Me that bears no fruit, while every branch that does bear fruit He prunes, that it may bear more fruit. Abide in Me, and I in you. As the branch cannot bear fruit of itself, unless it abides in the vine, neither can you, unless you abide in Me." (John 15:1-2,4)

READING

Slowly read the Scripture passage several times.

MEDITATION

Take some time to reflect on the words and phrases in the text. Which words, phrases, or images speak most to you?

PRAYER

Offer the internalized passage back to God in the form of a personalized prayer of adoration, confession, renewal, petition, intercession, affirmation, or thanksgiving.

CONTEMPLATION

What word or image captures the spirit of the passage for you?

Take a few minutes to present yourself before God in silence and yieldedness. When your mind wanders, center yourself by returning to the spirit of the passage.

SCRIPTURE

"As the Father has loved Me, so have I loved you; abide in My love. If you keep My commandments, you will abide in My love, just as I have kept My Father's commandments and abide in His love. I have told you these things so that My joy may be in you and that your joy may be full." (John 15:9-11)

READING

Slowly read the Scripture passage several times.

MEDITATION

Take some time to reflect on the words and phrases in the text. Which words, phrases, or images speak most to you?

PRAYER

Offer the internalized passage back to God in the form of a personalized prayer of adoration, confession, renewal, petition, intercession, affirmation, or thanksgiving.

CONTEMPLATION

What word or image captures the spirit of the passage for you?

Take a few minutes to present yourself before God in silence and yieldedness. When your mind wanders, center yourself by returning to the spirit of the passage.

SCRIPTURE

May I rejoice in my tribulations, knowing that tribulation produces perseverance; and perseverance, character; and character, hope. And hope does not disappoint, because the love of God has been poured out into my heart through the Holy Spirit who was given to me. (Romans 5:3-5)

READING

Slowly read the Scripture passage several times.

MEDITATION

Take some time to reflect on the words and phrases in the text.
Which words, phrases, or images speak most to you?

PRAYER

Offer the internalized passage back to God in the form of a personalized prayer of adoration, confession, renewal, petition, intercession, affirmation, or thanksgiving.

CONTEMPLATION

What word or image captures the spirit of the passage for you?

Take a few minutes to present yourself before God in silence and yieldedness. When your mind wanders, center yourself by returning to the spirit of the passage.

SCRIPTURE

There is now no condemnation for those who are in Christ Jesus, because the law of the Spirit of life in Christ Jesus has set me free from the law of sin and death. (Romans 8:1-2)

READING

Slowly read the Scripture passage several times.

MEDITATION

Take some time to reflect on the words and phrases in the text.
Which words, phrases, or images speak most to you?

PRAYER

Offer the internalized passage back to God in the form of a personalized prayer of adoration, confession, renewal, petition, intercession, affirmation, or thanksgiving.

CONTEMPLATION

What word or image captures the spirit of the passage for you?

Take a few minutes to present yourself before God in silence and yieldedness. When your mind wanders, center yourself by returning to the spirit of the passage.

SCRIPTURE

Those who live according to the flesh set their minds on the things of the flesh; but those who live according to the Spirit set their minds on the things of the Spirit. The mind of the flesh is death, but the mind of the Spirit is life and peace. (Romans 8:5-6)

READING

Slowly read the Scripture passage several times.

MEDITATION

Take some time to reflect on the words and phrases in the text. Which words, phrases, or images speak most to you?

PRAYER

Offer the internalized passage back to God in the form of a personalized prayer of adoration, confession, renewal, petition, intercession, affirmation, or thanksgiving.

CONTEMPLATION

What word or image captures the spirit of the passage for you?

Take a few minutes to present yourself before God in silence and yieldedness. When your mind wanders, center yourself by returning to the spirit of the passage.

SCRIPTURE

The Spirit helps me in my weakness, for I do not know what I ought to pray for, but the Spirit Himself intercedes for me with groans that words cannot express. And He who searches the heart knows the mind of the Spirit, because the Spirit intercedes for the saints according to the will of God. (Romans 8:26-27)

READING

Slowly read the Scripture passage several times.

MEDITATION

Take some time to reflect on the words and phrases in the text.
Which words, phrases, or images speak most to you?

PRAYER

Offer the internalized passage back to God in the form of a personalized prayer of adoration, confession, renewal, petition, intercession, affirmation, or thanksgiving.

CONTEMPLATION

What word or image captures the spirit of the passage for you?

Take a few minutes to present yourself before God in silence and yieldedness. When your mind wanders, center yourself by returning to the spirit of the passage.

SCRIPTURE

I am convinced that neither death nor life, nor angels nor principalities, nor things present nor things to come, nor powers, nor height nor depth, nor anything else in all creation, will be able to separate us from the love of God that is in Christ Jesus our Lord. (Romans 8:38-39)

READING

Slowly read the Scripture passage several times.

MEDITATION

Take some time to reflect on the words and phrases in the text. Which words, phrases, or images speak most to you?

PRAYER

Offer the internalized passage back to God in the form of a personalized prayer of adoration, confession, renewal, petition, intercession, affirmation, or thanksgiving.

CONTEMPLATION

What word or image captures the spirit of the passage for you?

Take a few minutes to present yourself before God in silence and yieldedness. When your mind wanders, center yourself by returning to the spirit of the passage.

SCRIPTURE

I urge you therefore, brethren, in view of God's mercy, to present your bodies as a living sacrifice, holy and pleasing to God, which is your reasonable service. And do not be conformed to the pattern of this world but be transformed by the renewing of your mind, that you may prove that the will of God is good and acceptable and perfect. (Romans 12:1-2)

READING

Slowly read the Scripture passage several times.

MEDITATION

Take some time to reflect on the words and phrases in the text. Which words, phrases, or images speak most to you?

PRAYER

Offer the internalized passage back to God in the form of a personalized prayer of adoration, confession, renewal, petition, intercession, affirmation, or thanksgiving.

CONTEMPLATION

What word or image captures the spirit of the passage for you?

Take a few minutes to present yourself before God in silence and yieldedness. When your mind wanders, center yourself by returning to the spirit of the passage.

SCRIPTURE

The foolishness of God is wiser than men, and the weakness of God is stronger than men. But God chose the foolish things of the world to shame the wise, and God chose the weak things of the world to shame the strong; and the lowly things of this world and the despised things God has chosen, and the things that are not, to nullify the things that are, so that no one may boast before Him. (1 Corinthians 1:25, 27-29)

READING

Slowly read the Scripture passage several times.

MEDITATION

Take some time to reflect on the words and phrases in the text. Which words, phrases, or images speak most to you?

PRAYER

Offer the internalized passage back to God in the form of a personalized prayer of adoration, confession, renewal, petition, intercession, affirmation, or thanksgiving.

CONTEMPLATION

What word or image captures the spirit of the passage for you?

Take a few minutes to present yourself before God in silence and yieldedness. When your mind wanders, center yourself by returning to the spirit of the passage.

SCRIPTURE

Love is patient, love is kind, it does not envy; love does not boast, it is not arrogant, it does not behave rudely; it does not seek its own, it is not provoked, it keeps no record of wrongs; it does not rejoice in unrighteousness but rejoices with the truth; it bears all things, believes all things, hopes all things, endures all things. Love never fails. (1 Corinthians 13:4-8)

READING

Slowly read the Scripture passage several times.

MEDITATION

Take some time to reflect on the words and phrases in the text.
Which words, phrases, or images speak most to you?

PRAYER

Offer the internalized passage back to God in the form of a personalized prayer of adoration, confession, renewal, petition, intercession, affirmation, or thanksgiving.

CONTEMPLATION

What word or image captures the spirit of the passage for you?

Take a few minutes to present yourself before God in silence and yieldedness. When your mind wanders, center yourself by returning to the spirit of the passage.

SCRIPTURE

Thanks be to God, who gives us the victory through our Lord Jesus Christ.
Therefore let us be steadfast, immovable, abounding in the work of the
Lord, knowing that our labor in the Lord is not in vain.
(1 Corinthians 15:57-58)

READING

Slowly read the Scripture passage several times.

MEDITATION

Take some time to reflect on the words and phrases in the text.
Which words, phrases, or images speak most to you?

PRAYER

Offer the internalized passage back to God in the form of a personalized
prayer of adoration, confession, renewal, petition, intercession,
affirmation, or thanksgiving.

CONTEMPLATION

What word or image captures the spirit of the passage for you?

Take a few minutes to present yourself before God in silence and
yieldedness. When your mind wanders, center yourself by returning to
the spirit of the passage.

SCRIPTURE

Thanks be to God, who always leads us in triumph in Christ and through us spreads everywhere the fragrance of the knowledge of Him.
(2 Corinthians 2:14)

READING

Slowly read the Scripture passage several times.

MEDITATION

Take some time to reflect on the words and phrases in the text.
Which words, phrases, or images speak most to you?

PRAYER

Offer the internalized passage back to God in the form of a personalized prayer of adoration, confession, renewal, petition, intercession, affirmation, or thanksgiving.

CONTEMPLATION

What word or image captures the spirit of the passage for you?

Take a few minutes to present yourself before God in silence and yieldedness. When your mind wanders, center yourself by returning to the spirit of the passage.

SCRIPTURE

God, who said, "Let light shine out of darkness," made His light shine in our hearts to give us the light of the knowledge of the glory of God in the face of Christ. But we have this treasure in earthen vessels to show that this all-surpassing power is from God and not from us. (2 Corinthians 4:6-7)

READING

Slowly read the Scripture passage several times.

MEDITATION

Take some time to reflect on the words and phrases in the text.
Which words, phrases, or images speak most to you?

PRAYER

Offer the internalized passage back to God in the form of a personalized prayer of adoration, confession, renewal, petition, intercession, affirmation, or thanksgiving.

CONTEMPLATION

What word or image captures the spirit of the passage for you?

Take a few minutes to present yourself before God in silence and yieldedness. When your mind wanders, center yourself by returning to the spirit of the passage.

SCRIPTURE

Your grace is sufficient for me, for Your power is made perfect in weakness. Therefore, I will boast all the more gladly in my weaknesses, that the power of Christ may rest upon me. Therefore, I can be content in weaknesses, in insults, in hardships, in persecutions, in difficulties, for Christ's sake. For when I am weak, then I am strong. (2 Corinthians 12:9-10)

READING

Slowly read the Scripture passage several times.

MEDITATION

Take some time to reflect on the words and phrases in the text. Which words, phrases, or images speak most to you?

PRAYER

Offer the internalized passage back to God in the form of a personalized prayer of adoration, confession, renewal, petition, intercession, affirmation, or thanksgiving.

CONTEMPLATION

What word or image captures the spirit of the passage for you?

Take a few minutes to present yourself before God in silence and yieldedness. When your mind wanders, center yourself by returning to the spirit of the passage.

SCRIPTURE

Through the law I died to the law so that I might live for God. I have been crucified with Christ; and it is no longer I who live, but Christ lives in me; and the life which I now live in the flesh, I live by faith in the Son of God, who loved me and gave Himself for me. To me, to live is Christ and to die is gain. (Galatians 2:19-20; Philippians 1:21)

READING

Slowly read the Scripture passage several times.

MEDITATION

Take some time to reflect on the words and phrases in the text.
Which words, phrases, or images speak most to you?

PRAYER

Offer the internalized passage back to God in the form of a personalized prayer of adoration, confession, renewal, petition, intercession, affirmation, or thanksgiving.

CONTEMPLATION

What word or image captures the spirit of the passage for you?

Take a few minutes to present yourself before God in silence and yieldedness. When your mind wanders, center yourself by returning to the spirit of the passage.

SCRIPTURE

The works of the flesh are evident, which are: immorality, impurity, sensuality, idolatry, sorcery, hatred, discord, jealousy, fits of rage, selfish ambition, dissensions, factions, envyings, drunkenness, revelries, and the like. Those who practice such things will not inherit the kingdom of God. But the fruit of the Spirit is love, joy, peace, patience, kindness, goodness, faithfulness, gentleness, self-control; against such things there is no law. (Galatians 5:19-23)

READING

Slowly read the Scripture passage several times.

MEDITATION

Take some time to reflect on the words and phrases in the text. Which words, phrases, or images speak most to you?

PRAYER

Offer the internalized passage back to God in the form of a personalized prayer of adoration, confession, renewal, petition, intercession, affirmation, or thanksgiving.

CONTEMPLATION

What word or image captures the spirit of the passage for you?

Take a few minutes to present yourself before God in silence and yieldedness. When your mind wanders, center yourself by returning to the spirit of the passage.

SCRIPTURE

May the God of our Lord Jesus Christ, the Father of glory, give you a spirit of wisdom and of revelation in the full knowledge of Him, and may the eyes of your heart be enlightened, in order that you may know what is the hope of His calling, what are the riches of His glorious inheritance in the saints, and what is the incomparable greatness of His power toward us who believe. (Ephesians 1:17-19)

READING

Slowly read the Scripture passage several times.

MEDITATION

Take some time to reflect on the words and phrases in the text. Which words, phrases, or images speak most to you?

PRAYER

Offer the internalized passage back to God in the form of a personalized prayer of adoration, confession, renewal, petition, intercession, affirmation, or thanksgiving.

CONTEMPLATION

What word or image captures the spirit of the passage for you?

Take a few minutes to present yourself before God in silence and yieldedness. When your mind wanders, center yourself by returning to the spirit of the passage.

SCRIPTURE

May God grant you, according to the riches of His glory, to be strengthened with power through His Spirit in your inner being, so that Christ may dwell in your hearts through faith. And may you, being rooted and grounded in love, be able to comprehend with all the saints what is the width and length and height and depth of the love of Christ, and to know this love that surpasses knowledge, that you may be filled to all the fullness of God. (Ephesians 3:16-19)

READING

Slowly read the Scripture passage several times.

MEDITATION

Take some time to reflect on the words and phrases in the text. Which words, phrases, or images speak most to you?

PRAYER

Offer the internalized passage back to God in the form of a personalized prayer of adoration, confession, renewal, petition, intercession, affirmation, or thanksgiving.

CONTEMPLATION

What word or image captures the spirit of the passage for you?

Take a few minutes to present yourself before God in silence and yieldedness. When your mind wanders, center yourself by returning to the spirit of the passage.

SCRIPTURE

With regard to my former way of life, may I put off my old self, which is being corrupted by its deceitful desires, and be renewed in the spirit of my mind; and may I put on the new self, which was created according to God in righteousness and true holiness. (Ephesians 4:22-24)

READING

Slowly read the Scripture passage several times.

MEDITATION

Take some time to reflect on the words and phrases in the text. Which words, phrases, or images speak most to you?

PRAYER

Offer the internalized passage back to God in the form of a personalized prayer of adoration, confession, renewal, petition, intercession, affirmation, or thanksgiving.

CONTEMPLATION

What word or image captures the spirit of the passage for you?

Take a few minutes to present yourself before God in silence and yieldedness. When your mind wanders, center yourself by returning to the spirit of the passage.

SCRIPTURE

I was once darkness, but now I am light in the Lord. May I walk as a child of light (for the fruit of the light consists in all goodness and righteousness and truth), learning what is pleasing to the Lord. (Ephesians 5:8-10)

READING

Slowly read the Scripture passage several times.

MEDITATION

Take some time to reflect on the words and phrases in the text. Which words, phrases, or images speak most to you?

PRAYER

Offer the internalized passage back to God in the form of a personalized prayer of adoration, confession, renewal, petition, intercession, affirmation, or thanksgiving.

CONTEMPLATION

What word or image captures the spirit of the passage for you?

Take a few minutes to present yourself before God in silence and yieldedness. When your mind wanders, center yourself by returning to the spirit of the passage.

SCRIPTURE

May your love abound more and more in full knowledge and depth of insight, so that you may be able to approve the things that are excellent, in order to be sincere and blameless until the day of Christ—having been filled with the fruit of righteousness that comes through Jesus Christ, to the glory and praise of God. (Philippians 1:9-11)

READING

Slowly read the Scripture passage several times.

MEDITATION

Take some time to reflect on the words and phrases in the text. Which words, phrases, or images speak most to you?

PRAYER

Offer the internalized passage back to God in the form of a personalized prayer of adoration, confession, renewal, petition, intercession, affirmation, or thanksgiving.

CONTEMPLATION

What word or image captures the spirit of the passage for you?

Take a few minutes to present yourself before God in silence and yieldedness. When your mind wanders, center yourself by returning to the spirit of the passage.

SCRIPTURE

Whatever was gain to me I now consider loss for the sake of Christ. What is more, I consider all things loss compared to the surpassing greatness of knowing Christ Jesus my Lord, for whose sake I have suffered the loss of all things and consider them rubbish, that I may gain Christ and be found in Him, not having a righteousness of my own that comes from the law, but that which is through faith in Christ—the righteousness that comes from God on the basis of faith. (Philippians 3:7-9)

READING

Slowly read the Scripture passage several times.

MEDITATION

Take some time to reflect on the words and phrases in the text. Which words, phrases, or images speak most to you?

PRAYER

Offer the internalized passage back to God in the form of a personalized prayer of adoration, confession, renewal, petition, intercession, affirmation, or thanksgiving.

CONTEMPLATION

What word or image captures the spirit of the passage for you?

Take a few minutes to present yourself before God in silence and yieldedness. When your mind wanders, center yourself by returning to the spirit of the passage.

SCRIPTURE

I have not been made perfect, but I press on to lay hold of that for which Christ Jesus also laid hold of me. I do not consider myself yet to have attained it, but one thing I do: forgetting what is behind and stretching forward to what is ahead, I press on toward the goal to win the prize of the upward call of God in Christ Jesus. (Philippians 3:12-14)

READING

Slowly read the Scripture passage several times.

MEDITATION

Take some time to reflect on the words and phrases in the text. Which words, phrases, or images speak most to you?

PRAYER

Offer the internalized passage back to God in the form of a personalized prayer of adoration, confession, renewal, petition, intercession, affirmation, or thanksgiving.

CONTEMPLATION

What word or image captures the spirit of the passage for you?

Take a few minutes to present yourself before God in silence and yieldedness. When your mind wanders, center yourself by returning to the spirit of the passage.

SCRIPTURE

Be anxious for nothing, but in everything by prayer and petition with thanksgiving, let your requests be known to God. And the peace of God, which transcends all understanding, will guard your hearts and your minds in Christ Jesus. (Philippians 4:6-7)

READING

Slowly read the Scripture passage several times.

MEDITATION

Take some time to reflect on the words and phrases in the text. Which words, phrases, or images speak most to you?

PRAYER

Offer the internalized passage back to God in the form of a personalized prayer of adoration, confession, renewal, petition, intercession, affirmation, or thanksgiving.

CONTEMPLATION

What word or image captures the spirit of the passage for you?

Take a few minutes to present yourself before God in silence and yieldedness. When your mind wanders, center yourself by returning to the spirit of the passage.

SCRIPTURE

Whatever is true, whatever is noble, whatever is right, whatever is pure, whatever is lovely, whatever is of good report—if anything is excellent or praiseworthy—may we think about such things. The things we have learned and received and heard and seen in those who walk with Christ we will practice, and the God of peace will be with us. (Philippians 4:8-9)

READING

Slowly read the Scripture passage several times.

MEDITATION

Take some time to reflect on the words and phrases in the text. Which words, phrases, or images speak most to you?

PRAYER

Offer the internalized passage back to God in the form of a personalized prayer of adoration, confession, renewal, petition, intercession, affirmation, or thanksgiving.

CONTEMPLATION

What word or image captures the spirit of the passage for you?

Take a few minutes to present yourself before God in silence and yieldedness. When your mind wanders, center yourself by returning to the spirit of the passage.

SCRIPTURE

May I learn to be content in whatever circumstances I am. Whether I am abased or in abundance, whether I am filled or hungry, let me learn the secret of being content in any and every situation. I can do all things through Him who strengthens me. (Philippians 4:11-13)

READING

Slowly read the Scripture passage several times.

MEDITATION

Take some time to reflect on the words and phrases in the text. Which words, phrases, or images speak most to you?

PRAYER

Offer the internalized passage back to God in the form of a personalized prayer of adoration, confession, renewal, petition, intercession, affirmation, or thanksgiving.

CONTEMPLATION

What word or image captures the spirit of the passage for you?

Take a few minutes to present yourself before God in silence and yieldedness. When your mind wanders, center yourself by returning to the spirit of the passage.

SCRIPTURE

*May God fill you with the knowledge of His will through all spiritual
wisdom and understanding, so that you may walk worthy of the Lord and
please Him in every way, bearing fruit in every good work, and growing
in the knowledge of God; strengthened with all power according to His
glorious might, so that you will have great endurance and patience
with joy.* (Colossians 1:9-11)

READING

Slowly read the Scripture passage several times.

MEDITATION

Take some time to reflect on the words and phrases in the text.
Which words, phrases, or images speak most to you?

PRAYER

Offer the internalized passage back to God in the form of a personalized
prayer of adoration, confession, renewal, petition, intercession,
affirmation, or thanksgiving.

CONTEMPLATION

What word or image captures the spirit of the passage for you?

Take a few minutes to present yourself before God in silence and
yieldedness. When your mind wanders, center yourself by returning to
the spirit of the passage.

SCRIPTURE

The Father has qualified us to share in the inheritance of the saints in the light. For He has rescued us from the dominion of darkness and brought us into the kingdom of His beloved Son, in whom we have redemption, the forgiveness of sins. (Colossians 1:12-14)

READING

Slowly read the Scripture passage several times.

MEDITATION

Take some time to reflect on the words and phrases in the text. Which words, phrases, or images speak most to you?

PRAYER

Offer the internalized passage back to God in the form of a personalized prayer of adoration, confession, renewal, petition, intercession, affirmation, or thanksgiving.

CONTEMPLATION

What word or image captures the spirit of the passage for you?

Take a few minutes to present yourself before God in silence and yieldedness. When your mind wanders, center yourself by returning to the spirit of the passage.

SCRIPTURE

Just as you received Christ Jesus the Lord, so walk in Him, rooted and built up in Him, and established in the faith, as you were taught, and abounding in thanksgiving. (Colossians 2:6-7)

READING

Slowly read the Scripture passage several times.

MEDITATION

Take some time to reflect on the words and phrases in the text. Which words, phrases, or images speak most to you?

PRAYER

Offer the internalized passage back to God in the form of a personalized prayer of adoration, confession, renewal, petition, intercession, affirmation, or thanksgiving.

CONTEMPLATION

What word or image captures the spirit of the passage for you?

Take a few minutes to present yourself before God in silence and yieldedness. When your mind wanders, center yourself by returning to the spirit of the passage.

SCRIPTURE

You have put off the old self with its practices and have put on the new self, who is being renewed in full knowledge according to the image of its Creator. (Colossians 3:9-10)

READING

Slowly read the Scripture passage several times.

MEDITATION

Take some time to reflect on the words and phrases in the text. Which words, phrases, or images speak most to you?

PRAYER

Offer the internalized passage back to God in the form of a personalized prayer of adoration, confession, renewal, petition, intercession, affirmation, or thanksgiving.

CONTEMPLATION

What word or image captures the spirit of the passage for you?

Take a few minutes to present yourself before God in silence and yieldedness. When your mind wanders, center yourself by returning to the spirit of the passage.

SCRIPTURE

As those who have been chosen of God, holy and beloved, put on a heart
of compassion, kindness, humility, gentleness, and patience, bearing with
others and forgiving others even as the Lord forgave you; and above all these
things, put on love, which is the bond of perfection. (Colossians 3:12-14)

READING

Slowly read the Scripture passage several times.

MEDITATION

Take some time to reflect on the words and phrases in the text.
Which words, phrases, or images speak most to you?

PRAYER

Offer the internalized passage back to God in the form of a personalized
prayer of adoration, confession, renewal, petition, intercession,
affirmation, or thanksgiving.

CONTEMPLATION

What word or image captures the spirit of the passage for you?

Take a few minutes to present yourself before God in silence and
yieldedness. When your mind wanders, center yourself by returning to
the spirit of the passage.

SCRIPTURE

This is the will of God, your sanctification, that you abstain from immorality and learn to possess your own vessel in sanctification and honor. For God did not call us to be impure, but to live a holy life. (1 Thessalonians 4:3-4, 7)

READING

Slowly read the Scripture passage several times.

MEDITATION

Take some time to reflect on the words and phrases in the text.
Which words, phrases, or images speak most to you?

PRAYER

Offer the internalized passage back to God in the form of a personalized prayer of adoration, confession, renewal, petition, intercession, affirmation, or thanksgiving.

CONTEMPLATION

What word or image captures the spirit of the passage for you?

Take a few minutes to present yourself before God in silence and yieldedness. When your mind wanders, center yourself by returning to the spirit of the passage.

SCRIPTURE

Rejoice always, pray without ceasing, and give thanks in all circumstances, for this is God's will for you in Christ Jesus. (1 Thessalonians 5:16-18)

READING

Slowly read the Scripture passage several times.

MEDITATION

Take some time to reflect on the words and phrases in the text. Which words, phrases, or images speak most to you?

PRAYER

Offer the internalized passage back to God in the form of a personalized prayer of adoration, confession, renewal, petition, intercession, affirmation, or thanksgiving.

CONTEMPLATION

What word or image captures the spirit of the passage for you?

Take a few minutes to present yourself before God in silence and yieldedness. When your mind wanders, center yourself by returning to the spirit of the passage.

SCRIPTURE

Those who want to get rich fall into temptation and a snare and into many foolish and harmful desires that plunge people into ruin and destruction. For the love of money is a root of all kinds of evil, and some by longing for it have wandered from the faith and pierced themselves with many sorrows. But let us flee from these things, and pursue righteousness, godliness, faith, love, patience, and gentleness. (1 Timothy 6:9-11)

READING

Slowly read the Scripture passage several times.

MEDITATION

Take some time to reflect on the words and phrases in the text. Which words, phrases, or images speak most to you?

PRAYER

Offer the internalized passage back to God in the form of a personalized prayer of adoration, confession, renewal, petition, intercession, affirmation, or thanksgiving.

CONTEMPLATION

What word or image captures the spirit of the passage for you?

Take a few minutes to present yourself before God in silence and yieldedness. When your mind wanders, center yourself by returning to the spirit of the passage.

SCRIPTURE

May I be above reproach, blameless as a steward of God, not self-willed, not quick-tempered, not given to wine, not violent, not fond of dishonest gain, but hospitable, a lover of what is good, sensible, just, holy, and self-controlled. (Titus 1:6-8)

READING

Slowly read the Scripture passage several times.

MEDITATION

Take some time to reflect on the words and phrases in the text. Which words, phrases, or images speak most to you?

PRAYER

Offer the internalized passage back to God in the form of a personalized prayer of adoration, confession, renewal, petition, intercession, affirmation, or thanksgiving.

CONTEMPLATION

What word or image captures the spirit of the passage for you?

Take a few minutes to present yourself before God in silence and yieldedness. When your mind wanders, center yourself by returning to the spirit of the passage.

SCRIPTURE

The word of God is living and active and sharper than any double-edged sword, piercing even to the dividing of soul and spirit and of joints and marrow, and it judges the thoughts and attitudes of the heart. And there is no creature hidden from His sight, but everything is uncovered and laid bare before the eyes of Him to whom we must give account. (Hebrews 4:12-13)

READING

Slowly read the Scripture passage several times.

MEDITATION

Take some time to reflect on the words and phrases in the text. Which words, phrases, or images speak most to you?

PRAYER

Offer the internalized passage back to God in the form of a personalized prayer of adoration, confession, renewal, petition, intercession, affirmation, or thanksgiving.

CONTEMPLATION

What word or image captures the spirit of the passage for you?

Take a few minutes to present yourself before God in silence and yieldedness. When your mind wanders, center yourself by returning to the spirit of the passage.

SCRIPTURE

Our hope in God is an anchor of our soul, both sure and steadfast, and it enters the inner sanctuary behind the veil, where Jesus the forerunner has entered on our behalf, having become a high priest forever, according to the order of Melchizedek. (Hebrews 6:19-20)

READING

Slowly read the Scripture passage several times.

MEDITATION

Take some time to reflect on the words and phrases in the text. Which words, phrases, or images speak most to you?

PRAYER

Offer the internalized passage back to God in the form of a personalized prayer of adoration, confession, renewal, petition, intercession, affirmation, or thanksgiving.

CONTEMPLATION

What word or image captures the spirit of the passage for you?

Take a few minutes to present yourself before God in silence and yieldedness. When your mind wanders, center yourself by returning to the spirit of the passage.

SCRIPTURE

Since we have a great cloud of witnesses surrounding us, let us also lay aside every impediment and the sin that so easily entangles, and run with endurance the race that is set before us, fixing our eyes on Jesus, the author and perfecter of faith, who for the joy set before Him endured the cross, despising the shame, and sat down at the right hand of the throne of God. For consider Him who endured such hostility from sinners, so that you will not grow weary and lose heart. (Hebrews 12:1-3)

READING

Slowly read the Scripture passage several times.

MEDITATION

Take some time to reflect on the words and phrases in the text.
Which words, phrases, or images speak most to you?

PRAYER

Offer the internalized passage back to God in the form of a personalized prayer of adoration, confession, renewal, petition, intercession, affirmation, or thanksgiving.

CONTEMPLATION

What word or image captures the spirit of the passage for you?

Take a few minutes to present yourself before God in silence and yieldedness. When your mind wanders, center yourself by returning to the spirit of the passage.

S CRIPTURE

You have come to Mount Zion, to the heavenly Jerusalem, the city of the living God, and to myriads of angels, to the assembly and church of the firstborn, who are enrolled in heaven, and to God, the judge of all men, and to the spirits of righteous people made perfect, and to Jesus the mediator of a new covenant, and to the sprinkled blood that speaks better things than the blood of Abel. (Hebrews 12:22-24)

R EADING

Slowly read the Scripture passage several times.

M EDITATION

Take some time to reflect on the words and phrases in the text.
Which words, phrases, or images speak most to you?

P RAYER

Offer the internalized passage back to God in the form of a personalized prayer of adoration, confession, renewal, petition, intercession, affirmation, or thanksgiving.

C ONTEMPLATION

What word or image captures the spirit of the passage for you?

Take a few minutes to present yourself before God in silence and yieldedness. When your mind wanders, center yourself by returning to the spirit of the passage.

SCRIPTURE

Everyone should be quick to hear, slow to speak, and slow to anger, for the anger of man does not produce the righteousness of God. (James 1:19-20)

READING

Slowly read the Scripture passage several times.

MEDITATION

Take some time to reflect on the words and phrases in the text.
Which words, phrases, or images speak most to you?

PRAYER

Offer the internalized passage back to God in the form of a personalized prayer of adoration, confession, renewal, petition, intercession, affirmation, or thanksgiving.

CONTEMPLATION

What word or image captures the spirit of the passage for you?

Take a few minutes to present yourself before God in silence and yieldedness. When your mind wanders, center yourself by returning to the spirit of the passage.

SCRIPTURE

Prove yourselves doers of the word and not merely hearers who deceive themselves. For if anyone is a hearer of the word and not a doer, he is like a man who looks at his natural face in a mirror, and after looking at himself, goes away, and immediately forgets what kind of person he was. But the one who looks intently into the perfect law of freedom and continues in it and is not a forgetful hearer but a doer of the word, this one will be blessed in what he does. (James 1:22-25)

READING

Slowly read the Scripture passage several times.

MEDITATION

Take some time to reflect on the words and phrases in the text. Which words, phrases, or images speak most to you?

PRAYER

Offer the internalized passage back to God in the form of a personalized prayer of adoration, confession, renewal, petition, intercession, affirmation, or thanksgiving.

CONTEMPLATION

What word or image captures the spirit of the passage for you?

Take a few minutes to present yourself before God in silence and yieldedness. When your mind wanders, center yourself by returning to the spirit of the passage.

SCRIPTURE

You have been chosen according to the foreknowledge of God the Father, in sanctification of the Spirit, for obedience to Jesus Christ and sprinkling of His blood; may grace and peace be yours in abundance. (1 Peter 1:2)

READING

Slowly read the Scripture passage several times.

MEDITATION

Take some time to reflect on the words and phrases in the text.
Which words, phrases, or images speak most to you?

PRAYER

Offer the internalized passage back to God in the form of a personalized prayer of adoration, confession, renewal, petition, intercession, affirmation, or thanksgiving.

CONTEMPLATION

What word or image captures the spirit of the passage for you?

Take a few minutes to present yourself before God in silence and yieldedness. When your mind wanders, center yourself by returning to the spirit of the passage.

SCRIPTURE

You greatly rejoice in your salvation, though now for a little while, if necessary, you have been grieved by various trials, so that the proving of your faith, being much more precious than gold that perishes, even though refined by fire, may be found to result in praise, glory, and honor at the revelation of Jesus Christ. (1 Peter 1:6-7)

READING

Slowly read the Scripture passage several times.

MEDITATION

Take some time to reflect on the words and phrases in the text. Which words, phrases, or images speak most to you?

PRAYER

Offer the internalized passage back to God in the form of a personalized prayer of adoration, confession, renewal, petition, intercession, affirmation, or thanksgiving.

CONTEMPLATION

What word or image captures the spirit of the passage for you?

Take a few minutes to present yourself before God in silence and yieldedness. When your mind wanders, center yourself by returning to the spirit of the passage.

SCRIPTURE

Be diligent to add to your faith, virtue; and to virtue, knowledge; and to knowledge, self-control; and to self-control, perseverance; and to perseverance, godliness; and to godliness, brotherly kindness; and to brotherly kindness, love. For if these qualities are yours in increasing measure, they will keep you from being barren and unfruitful in the full knowledge of our Lord Jesus Christ. (2 Peter 1:5-8)

READING

Slowly read the Scripture passage several times.

MEDITATION

Take some time to reflect on the words and phrases in the text.
Which words, phrases, or images speak most to you?

PRAYER

Offer the internalized passage back to God in the form of a personalized prayer of adoration, confession, renewal, petition, intercession, affirmation, or thanksgiving.

CONTEMPLATION

What word or image captures the spirit of the passage for you?

Take a few minutes to present yourself before God in silence and yieldedness. When your mind wanders, center yourself by returning to the spirit of the passage.

SCRIPTURE

Do not love the world or the things in the world. If anyone loves the world, the love of the Father is not in him. For all that is in the world— the lust of the flesh, the lust of the eyes, and the pride of life—is not of the Father but of the world. And the world and its lusts are passing away, but the one who does the will of God abides forever. (1 John 2:15-17)

READING

Slowly read the Scripture passage several times.

MEDITATION

Take some time to reflect on the words and phrases in the text. Which words, phrases, or images speak most to you?

PRAYER

Offer the internalized passage back to God in the form of a personalized prayer of adoration, confession, renewal, petition, intercession, affirmation, or thanksgiving.

CONTEMPLATION

What word or image captures the spirit of the passage for you?

Take a few minutes to present yourself before God in silence and yieldedness. When your mind wanders, center yourself by returning to the spirit of the passage.

SCRIPTURE

See what manner of love the Father has lavished on us, that we should be called children of God—and we are! Therefore the world does not know us, because it did not know Him. Now we are children of God, and what we will be has not yet been revealed. We know that when He is revealed, we will be like Him, for we will see Him as He is. And everyone who has this hope in Him purifies himself, just as He is pure. (1 John 3:1-3)

READING

Slowly read the Scripture passage several times.

MEDITATION

Take some time to reflect on the words and phrases in the text.
Which words, phrases, or images speak most to you?

PRAYER

Offer the internalized passage back to God in the form of a personalized prayer of adoration, confession, renewal, petition, intercession, affirmation, or thanksgiving.

CONTEMPLATION

What word or image captures the spirit of the passage for you?

Take a few minutes to present yourself before God in silence and yieldedness. When your mind wanders, center yourself by returning to the spirit of the passage.

SCRIPTURE

To You who are able to keep me from falling and to present me before Your glorious presence faultless and with great joy—to the only God my Savior, through Jesus Christ my Lord, be glory, majesty, dominion, and authority, before all ages and now and forever. Amen. (Jude 24-25)

READING

Slowly read the Scripture passage several times.

MEDITATION

Take some time to reflect on the words and phrases in the text. Which words, phrases, or images speak most to you?

PRAYER

Offer the internalized passage back to God in the form of a personalized prayer of adoration, confession, renewal, petition, intercession, affirmation, or thanksgiving.

CONTEMPLATION

What word or image captures the spirit of the passage for you?

Take a few minutes to present yourself before God in silence and yieldedness. When your mind wanders, center yourself by returning to the spirit of the passage.

SCRIPTURE

The Holy City, new Jerusalem, will come down out of heaven from God, prepared as a bride adorned for her husband. A loud voice from the throne will say, "Behold, the tabernacle of God is with men, and He will dwell with them, and they will be His people, and God Himself will be with them and be their God, and He will wipe every tear from their eyes. There will be no more death or mourning or crying or pain, for the first things have passed away." He who is seated on the throne will say, "Behold, I make all things new." (Revelation 21:2-5)

READING

Slowly read the Scripture passage several times.

MEDITATION

Take some time to reflect on the words and phrases in the text.
Which words, phrases, or images speak most to you?

PRAYER

Offer the internalized passage back to God in the form of a personalized prayer of adoration, confession, renewal, petition, intercession, affirmation, or thanksgiving.

CONTEMPLATION

What word or image captures the spirit of the passage for you?

Take a few minutes to present yourself before God in silence and yieldedness. When your mind wanders, center yourself by returning to the spirit of the passage.

SCRIPTURE

There will no longer be any curse. The throne of God and of the Lamb will be in the new Jerusalem, and His servants will serve Him. They will see His face, and His name will be on their foreheads. And there will be no night there; they will not need the light of a lamp or the light of the sun, for the Lord God will give them light. And they shall reign for ever and ever. (Revelation 22:3-5)

READING

Slowly read the Scripture passage several times.

MEDITATION

Take some time to reflect on the words and phrases in the text. Which words, phrases, or images speak most to you?

PRAYER

Offer the internalized passage back to God in the form of a personalized prayer of adoration, confession, renewal, petition, intercession, affirmation, or thanksgiving.

CONTEMPLATION

What word or image captures the spirit of the passage for you?

Take a few minutes to present yourself before God in silence and yieldedness. When your mind wanders, center yourself by returning to the spirit of the passage.

WHERE TO GO FROM HERE

I trust that this ninety-day process has been meaningful and spiritually nourishing for you. Now that you have completed this journal of sacred readings, you should go back and read through the comments and prayers you have recorded. As you do this, be sure to mark the journal entries that strongly resonate with your spirit.

As I mentioned at the end of the introduction, it would be especially helpful for you to go through this process a second time and visit each of these passages once again. You will discover new things in the Scripture texts that you did not see the first time through. Use a different color of ink for your journal comments each time you revisit a passage.

I also encourage you to use the other journals in this *Reflections* series. *Historic Creeds: A Journal* moves through three historic creeds of the faith (the Apostles' Creed, the Nicene Creed, and the Athanasian Creed) and relates each element of these creeds to a Scripture text for sacred reading.

The Psalms: A Journal will enhance your devotional life as you meditate on and pray back to God ninety selections from the book of Psalms.

The Trinity: A Journal is designed to take you on a meditative journey through each of the three Persons of the divine Trinity by guiding you through thirty passages on the Father, thirty passages on the Son, and thirty passages on the Holy Spirit.

ABOUT THE AUTHOR

DR. KENNETH BOA is the president of Reflections Ministries. He has authored many books including *Pursuing Wisdom* and *The Art of Living Well* (both NavPress) and is a contributing editor to the *Open Bible*, the *Promise Keeper's Men's Study Bible*, and the *Leadership Bible*. Dr. Boa earned a bachelor's degree from Case Institute of Technology, a master's degree in theology from Dallas Theological Seminary, and doctoral degrees from both New York University and the University of Oxford. He resides in Atlanta, Georgia.

Kenneth Boa writes a free monthly teaching letter called *Reflections*. If you would like to be on the mailing list, call: 800-DRAW NEAR (800-372-9632).

CARRY YOUR BELIEF FROM YOUR HEAD TO YOUR HEART.

Historic Creeds

Since the early days of Christianity, the most vital tenets of the faith have been captured in a number of historic statements including the Apostles' Creed, the Nicene Creed, and the Athanasian Creed. More than dusty, ancient documents, these passionate declarations are deeply relevant to believers today. They will open your eyes to essential teachings and help you develop a deeper understanding of the truths upon which Christ's church was built.

Historic Creeds (Kenneth Boa) $10